GREEN

LYRIC & CHORD SONGBOOK

T0059146

Produced by
Alfred Music Publishing Co., Inc.
P.O. Box 10003
Van Nuys, CA 91410-0003
alfred.com

Printed in USA.

ISBN-10: 0-7390-8034-2
ISBN-13: 978-0-7390-8034-4

Cover Photos
Green Day: © Bob Gruen • Wall: © iStockphoto.com / neoellis

 Alfred Cares. Contents printed on 100% recycled paper.

Contents

TITLE	RELEASE	PAGE
16	1,039/Smoothed Out Slappy Hours	4
21 Guns	21st Century Breakdown	7
21st Century Breakdown	21st Century Breakdown	10
80	Kerplunk	14
86	Insomniac	16
1,000 Hours	1,039/Smoothed Out Slappy Hours	18
2,000 Light Years Away	Kerplunk	20
All by Myself	Dookie	22
American Eulogy	21st Century Breakdown	26

  A. Mass Hysteria

  B. Modern World

American Idiot	American Idiot	23
Are We the Waiting	American Idiot	30
At the Library	1,039/Smoothed Out Slappy Hours	34
Basket Case	Dookie	36
Before the Lobotomy	21st Century Breakdown	31
Boulevard of Broken Dreams	American Idiot	38
Brain Stew	Insomniac	42
Burnout	Dookie	44
Christie Road	Kerplunk	46
Coming Clean	Dookie	41
Dominated Love Slave	Kerplunk	48
Don't Leave Me	1,039/Smoothed Out Slappy Hours	50
East Jesus Nowhere	21st Century Breakdown	52
Extraordinary Girl	American Idiot	56
F.O.D.	Dookie	58
Geek Stink Breath	Insomniac	60
Going to Pasalacqua	1,039/Smoothed Out Slappy Hours	62
Good Riddance (Time of Your Life)	Nimrod	68
Green Day	1,039/Smoothed Out Slappy Hours	65
The Grouch	Nimrod	70
Hitchin' a Ride	Nimrod	72
Holiday	American Idiot	74
Homecoming	American Idiot	80

  I. The Death of St. Jimmy

  II. East 12th St.

  III. Nobody Likes You

  IV. Rock and Roll Girlfriend

  V. We're Coming Home Again

Horseshoes and Handgrenades	21st Century Breakdown	77
Jaded	Insomniac	86
J.A.R. (Jason Andrew Relva)	*Angus* soundtrack	88

Jesus of Suburbia .... American Idiot 91
  I. Jesus of Suburbia
  II. City of the Damned
  III. I Don't Care
  IV. Dearly Beloved
  V. Tales of Another Broken Home
King for a Day .... Nimrod 98
Know Your Enemy .... 21st Century Breakdown 104
Last Night on Earth .... 21st Century Breakdown 106
Last of the American Girls .... 21st Century Breakdown 101
Longview .... Dookie 108
Macy's Day Parade .... Warning 110
Maria .... International Superhits! 112
Minority .... Warning 116
Murder City .... 21st Century Breakdown 114
Nice Guys Finish Last .... Nimrod 119
One for the Razorbacks .... Kerplunk 122
The One I Want .... 1,039/Smoothed Out Slappy Hours 124
One of My Lies .... Kerplunk 126
Only of You .... 1,039/Smoothed Out Slappy Hours 128
Paper Lanterns .... 1,039/Smoothed Out Slappy Hours 130
Peacemaker .... 21st Century Breakdown 132
Private Ale .... Kerplunk 138
Restless Heart Syndrome .... 21st Century Breakdown 135
See the Light .... 21st Century Breakdown 140
She .... Dookie 142
She's a Rebel .... American Idiot 144
St. Jimmy .... American Idiot 146
The Static Age .... 21st Century Breakdown 149
Stuck with Me .... Insomniac 152
Uptight .... Nimrod 154
¡Viva la Gloria! .... 21st Century Breakdown 156
¿Viva la Gloria? (Little Girl) .... 21st Century Breakdown 159
Waiting .... Warning 162
Wake Me Up When September Ends .... American Idiot 168
Walking Contradiction .... Insomniac 170
Warning .... Warning 165
Welcome to Paradise .... Dookie 172
When I Come Around .... Dookie 174
Who Wrote Holden Caulfield? .... Kerplunk 176

16

Lyrics by BILLIE JOE
Music by GREEN DAY

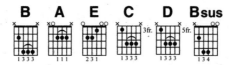

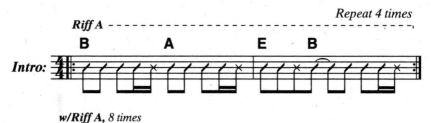

w/Riff A, *8 times*

B

Verse 1: Ev'ry   night, I dream the same   dream

Of getting older and older all the time.

I   ask you now · what does this mean?

Are all these problems just in my mind?

Things are easy when you're a   child.

But now these pressures have dropped on my head.

The length I've gone are just long miles.

Would they be shorter if I were dead?

Chorus:

C   **D**   **Bsus**
Ev'ry   time   I   look   in my past,

C   **D**   **Bsus**
I always wish   I was   there.

C   **D**   **Bsus**
I wish   my youth would forever last.

C   **D**   **Bsus**
Why   are these   times   so unfair?

w/Riff A, 2 times

Interlude: | B   A | E   B | B   A | E   B   ‖

w/Riff A, 8 times

B

Verse 2:   Look   at my friends and see what they've done.

Ask myself why they had to change.

I like them better when they were young.

Now all those   times   are   rearranged.

I look down and stand there and cry.

Nothing ever will be the same.

The sun is rising, now I ask why.

The clouds now fall and here comes the rain.

C   **D**   **Bsus**

Chorus: Ev'ry   time   I   look   in my past,

C   **D**   **Bsus**

I always wish I was there.

C   **D**   **Bsus**

I wish ·my   youth would forever last.

C   **D**   **Bsus**

Why   are these   times   so unfair?

Interlude:

Instrumental Chorus: *Repeat 4 times*

‖: C   D | Bsus   :‖

6

Verse 3:

w/Riff A, 8 times
B

Ev'ry   night,   I   dream   the same   dream

Of   getting   older   and older   all   the   time.

I   ask   you   now   what   does   this mean?

Are   all   these problems   just in   my   mind?

Things   are easy when   you're a   child.

But   now   these pressures   have dropped on   my head.

The   length I've   gone   are just   long   miles.

Would   they   be   shorter   if   I   were   dead?

Chorus:

      C   **D**   **Bsus**
Ev'ry   time   I   look   in   my   past,

      C   **D**   **Bsus**
I   always   wish   I   was   there.

      C   **D**   **Bsus**
I   wish   my youth   would   forever last.

      C   **D**   **Bsus**
Why   are   these   times   so   unfair?

Instrumental Chorus: *Repeat 4 times*

‖: **C**   **D** | **Bsus**   :‖

Outro:

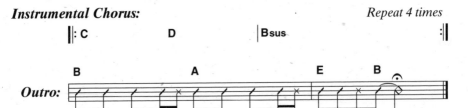

21 GUNS

Words and Music by
**BILLIE JOE, GREEN DAY,
DAVID BOWIE and JOHN PHILLIPS**

Dm B♭ F C A

Intro: | **4/4** **Dm**   **B♭** | **F**   **C** | **Dm**   **B♭** | **F**   **C** ‖

Verse 1:

Dm   **B♭**   **F**   **C**
Do you know what's worth fighting for,

Dm   **B♭**   **F**   **C**
When it's not worth dying for?

Dm   **B♭**   **F**   **C**
Does it take your breath away

                 B♭   **C**
And you feel yourself suffocating?

Verse 2:

Dm   **B♭**   **F**   **C**
Does the pain weigh out the pride?

Dm   **B♭**   **F**   **C**
And you look for a place to hide?

Dm   **B♭**   **F**   **C**
Did someone break your heart inside,

                 B♭   **C**
You're in ruins.

Chorus:

F   **C**   **Dm**   **C**   **B♭**
One, twenty - one guns, lay down your arms,

F   **C**
give up the fight.

F   **C**   **Dm**   **C**   **B♭**
One, twenty - one guns, throw up your arms

F   **C**   **B♭** **F** **C**
into the sky, you and I.

8

Verse 3:
Dm   B♭   F   C
When you're at the end of the road,

Dm   B♭   F   C
And you lost all sense of control.

Dm   B♭   F   C
And your thoughts have taken their toll,

      B♭   C
When your mind breaks the spirit of your soul.

Verse 4:
Dm   B♭   F   C
Your faith walks on broken glass,

Dm   B♭   F   C
And the hangover doesn't pass.

Dm   B♭ F   C   B♭ C
Nothing's ever built to last, You're in ruins.

Chorus:
F C   Dm C   B♭
One, twenty - one guns, lay down your arms,

F   C
give up the fight.

F C   Dm C   B♭
One, twenty - one guns, throw up your arms

F   C   B♭ F C
into the sky, you and I.

Bridge:
Dm   B♭   F   C
Did you try to live on your own,

Dm   B♭   F   A
When you burned down the house and home?

Dm   B♭   F   A
Did you stand too close to the fire?

     B♭   C   F
Like a liar looking for forgiveness from a stone.

Guitar Solo:
‖: F C |Dm C |B♭ F |C :‖ B♭   F |A   ‖

Interlude:

| Dm Bb | F C | Dm Bb | F C |

Verse 5:

Dm   Bb   F   C
When it's time to live and let die,

Dm   Bb   F C
And you can't get another try.

Dm   Bb   F   C
Something inside this heart has died,

       Bb C
You're in ruins.

Chorus:

F C   Dm C   Bb
One, twenty - one guns, lay down your arms,

F   C
give up the fight.

F C   Dm C   Bb
One, twenty - one guns, throw up your arms

F   C
into the sky.

F C   Dm C   Bb
One, twenty - one guns, lay down your arms,

F   C
give up the fight.

F C   Dm C   Bb
One, twenty - one guns, throw up your arms

F   C   Bb F C
into the sky, you and I.

21ST CENTURY BREAKDOWN

Lyrics by BILLIE JOE
Music by GREEN DAY

To match recording,
tune down 1/2 step:
⑥ = Eb   ③ = Gb
⑤ = Ab   ② = Bb
④ = Db   ① = Eb

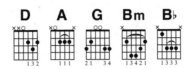

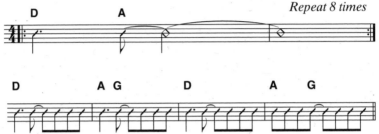

Verse 1:

D
Born into Nixon, I was raised in hell, (A) (G)

D
A welfare child where the teamsters dwelled. (A) (G)

D
The last one born and the first one to run, (A) (G)

D
My town was blind from refinery sun. (A) (G)

Pre-chorus:

Bm   G
My generation is zero,

Bm   G   A
I never made it as a working class hero.

Chorus:

D   A   G
Twenty-first century breakdown,

D   A   G
I once was lost but never was found.

D   A   G
I think I'm losing what's left of my mind

D   A   G
to the twentieth century deadline.

D   A G   D   A   G
Ooh.

             D   **A**   **G**

Verse 2:   I was   made of poison and blood,

             D   **A**   **G**

        Condemnation is what   I understood.

             D   **A**   **G**

        Video   games to the tower's fall,

             D   **A**   **G**

        Homeland security could   kill us all.

        Bm   **G**

Pre-chorus: My generation is   zero,

        Bm   **G**   **A**

        I never made it as a working class   hero.

       D   **A**   **G**

Chorus: Twenty - first   century breakdown,

           D   **A**   **G**

      I once was   lost   but   never was   found.

           D   **A**   **G**

      I think I'm   losing what's left   of my mind

              D   **A**   **G**

    to the twentieth century deadline.

           A

Interlude:

Repeat 4 times

       A   **D**

Verse 3: We are the class of, the class of 'thirteen,

       A   **D**

      Born in the year   of humility.

       A   **D**

      We are the desperate in the decline,

       A   **D**

      Raised by the bastards of nineteen-sixty - nine.

                                                              Repeat 4 times

Interlude: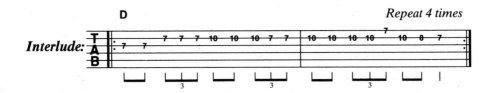

Verse 4:

    D   **G**   **A** **D**

My name   is   no one,   the long   lost son,

                            A

born   on the Fourth of July.

D   **G**   **A** **D**

Raised   in the era of heroes   and cons,

                          A

who   left me for dead   or alive.

D   **G**   **A** **D**

I   am a   nation, a   worker of pride.

                     A

My debt   to the status   quo.

      D   **G**   **A** **D**

The scars   on my hands and a means to an end

                     A

is   all that   I   have   to show.

                                                              Repeat 4 times
                                                                        G
Interlude: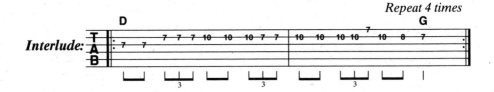

Verse 5:

    D   **G**   **A** **D**

I swallowed   my pride   and I   choked on my faith.

                        A

I've given   my heart   and my soul.

      D   **G**   **A** **D**

I've broken my fingers and lied through my teeth,

                    A

The pillar   of damage control.

    D   **G**   **A**   **D**
I've been to the edge and I've thrown the bouquet

                        A
of flowers left over the grave.

   D   **G**   **A** **D**
I sat in the waiting room, wasting my time

                      A
and waiting for Judgment Day.

      G   **A D**
Bridge: Praise liberty,

       G   **A D**
the "freedom to obey" is the

G   **A**   **D**
song   that   strangles me.

         G   **A** **G**   **A** **G**
Well, don't cross the line.

Interlude:

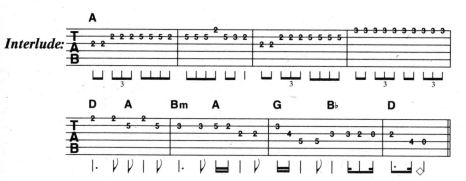

        D   **A**   **Bm**   **A**
Outro: Oh, dream, America, dream. I can't   even

G   **B♭**   **D**
sleep from light's early dawn.

             A   **Bm**   **A**
Oh, scream, America, scream. Believe what you

G   **B♭**   **(D)**
see   from   heroes and cons.

80

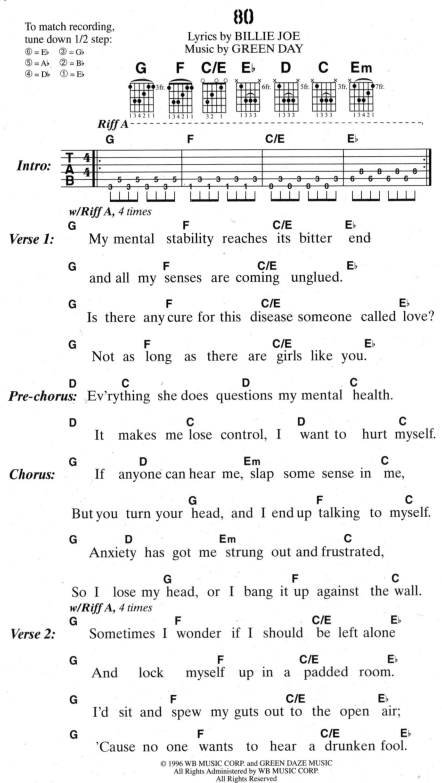

To match recording,
tune down 1/2 step:
⑥ = Eb   ③ = Gb
⑤ = Ab   ② = Bb
④ = Db   ① = Eb

Lyrics by BILLIE JOE
Music by GREEN DAY

Riff A

Intro:

w/Riff A, 4 times

Verse 1:
G .... F .... C/E .... Eb
My mental stability reaches its bitter end

G .... F .... C/E .... Eb
and all my senses are coming unglued.

G .... F .... C/E .... Eb
Is there any cure for this disease someone called love?

G .... F .... C/E .... Eb
Not as long as there are girls like you.

Pre-chorus:
D ...... C .... D C
Ev'rything she does questions my mental health.

D .... C .... D C
It makes me lose control, I   want to   hurt myself.

Chorus:
G ...... D .... Em C
If anyone can hear me, slap some sense in me,

G .... F C
But you turn your head, and I end up talking to myself.

G .... D .... Em C
Anxiety has got me strung out and frustrated,

G .... F C
So I lose my head, or I bang it up against the wall.

w/Riff A, 4 times

Verse 2:
G .... F .... C/E .... Eb
Sometimes I wonder if I should   be left alone

G .... F .... C/E .... Eb
And   lock   myself up in a padded room.

G .... F .... C/E .... Eb
I'd sit and spew my guts out to the open air;

G .... F .... C/E .... Eb
'Cause no one wants   to hear a drunken fool.

Pre-chorus:
D   C   D   C
Ev'rything she does questions my mental health.

   D   C   D   C
It makes me lose control, I just can't trust myself.

Chorus:
 G   D   Em   C
If anyone can hear me, slap some sense in me,

              G   F   C
But you turn your head, and I end up talking to myself.

 G   D   Em   C
Anxiety has got me strung out and frustrated,

           G   F   C
So I lose my head, or I bang it up against the wall.

Bridge:
C   D   G C G
I do not mind if this goes on,

C   D   G C G
'Cause now it seems I'm too far gone.

C   D   G   C
I must admit that I enjoy myself.

                D   G
Adi, please keep taking me away.

Interlude: *Riff B* — — — — — — — — — — — — — — — — *Repeat 4 times*

G   F   C/E   E♭

```
T|------3---3------|---3---3------|---3---3------|---0---0------|
A|--5---5---5------|3--3---3---3--|2--2---2---2--|1--1---1---1--|
B|0-----0---0---0--|-----0--------|--------------|--------------|
```

Pre-chorus:
D   C   D   C
Ev'rything she does questions my mental health.

   D   C   D   C
It makes me lose control, I just can't trust myself.

Chorus:
 G   D   Em   C
If anyone can hear me, slap some sense in me,

              G   F   C
But you turn your head, and I end up talking to myself.

 G   D   Em   C
Anxiety has got me strung out and frustrated,

           G   F   C
So I lose my head, or I bang it up against the wall.

w/Riff B   *Repeat and fade*

Outro: ‖: G | F | C/E | E♭   :‖

86

Lyrics by BILLIE JOE
Music by GREEN DAY

To match recording,
tune down 1/2 step:
⑥ = E♭   ③ = G♭
⑤ = A♭   ② = B♭
④ = D♭   ① = E♭

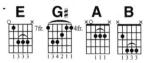

E   G♯   A   B

Intro: $\frac{4}{4}$

E   G♯   A

Verse 1:
E   B
What brings you around?

        A   E   A
Did you lose something the last time you were here?

E   B
You'll never find it now.

    A   E
It's buried deep within your identity.

Pre-chorus:
B   A
So, stand aside and let the next one pass.

B   A
Don't let the door kick you in the ass.

Chorus:
E   G♯   A
There's no return from Eighty Six.

E   G♯   A
There's no return from Eighty Six.

E   G♯   A
There's no return from Eighty Six.

E   G♯   A
There's no return from Eighty Six. Don't even try.

Verse 2:
E   B
Exit out the back

    A   E   A
And never show your head around again.

E   B
Purchase your ticket

    A   E
And quickly take the last train out of town.

Pre-chorus: **B**
So, stand aside and let the **A** next one pass.

B
Don't let the door kick you **A** in the ass.

Chorus: **E**   **G♯**
There's no return from   **A** Eighty Six.

E   **G♯**
There's no return from   **A** Eighty Six.

E   **G♯**
There's no return from   **A** Eighty Six.

E   **G♯**
There's no return from   **A** Eighty Six. Don't even try.

Interlude:

Repeat 4 times

Chorus: **E**   **G♯**
There's no return from   **A** Eighty Six.

E   **G♯**
There's no return from   **A** Eighty Six.

E   **G♯**
There's no return from   **A** Eighty Six.

E   **G♯**
There's no return from   **A** Eighty Six.

B **A**
Don't even try.

1,000 HOURS

Lyrics by BILLIE JOE
Music by GREEN DAY

To match recording,
tune down 1/2 step:
⑥ = E♭   ③ = G♭
⑤ = A♭   ② = B♭
④ = D♭   ① = E♭

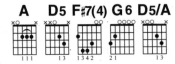

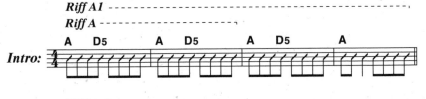

Riff A1 -

Riff A -

	A D5	A D5	A D5	A

Intro: 4/4

w/Riff A, 8 times

A

Verse 1: Starlit night, the moon is shinging bright,

You're the one that I need.

Up at your window, I see a shadow,

Silhouette of your grace.

Here's this flower I picked for all the hours

That you spent with me.

The one I love, that I've been dreaming of

Sailing across   the sea.

      F♯7(4)   G6   F♯7(4)

Chorus: Let my hands flow through your hair.

          G6   F♯7(4)

Moving closer, kiss we'll share.

          G6   F♯7(4)

Passionate love to be all night long.

                                w/Riff A1

          G6   A

We'll never break, as one too strong.

w/Riff A, *8 times*

A

Verse 2: Ah, nothing's more than what our love is for

As I kiss your cheek.

Oh, so softly hands flowing down my back,

A thousand hours I'll never leave.

Our romance is a love trance

And now we'll never part.

A thousand hours of such a love shower,

We'll never stop once we start.

F♯7(4)   **G6**   **F♯7(4)**
Chorus: Let my hands flow through your hair.

G6   **F♯7(4)**
Moving closer, kiss we'll share.

G6   **F♯7(4)**
Passionate love to be all night long.

w/Riff A1   *w/Riff A,* *2 times*
G6   **A**   **A**
We'll never break, as one too strong.

F♯7(4)   **G6**   **F♯7(4)**
Chorus: Let my hands flow through your hair.

G6   **F♯7(4)**
Moving closer, kiss we'll share.

G6   **F♯7(4)**
Passionate love to be all night long.

w/Riff A, *4 times*
G6   **A**
We'll never break, as one too strong.

Guitar *w/Riff A1*   *Repeat 4 times*
Solo: ‖: A   D5 | A   D5 | A   D5 | A   :‖

A   D5/A   A   D5/A   A   D5/A   A   D5/A   D5/A

Outro:

Strong.

2,000 LIGHT YEARS AWAY

Lyrics by BILLIE JOE
Music by GREEN DAY

To match recording,
tune down 1/2 step:
⑥ = E♭   ③ = G♭
⑤ = A♭   ② = B♭
④ = D♭   ① = E♭

B   G#m   F#   E

Repeat 4 times

Riff A -

Intro: B   G#m   F#

Verse 1:
　　B　　　F#
I sit alone in my bedroom　　staring at the walls.
　　　　　　　　　B　　　　　　　F#

　　B　　　F#
I've been up all damn night long.

　　B
My pulse is speeding.　　My love is yearning.
　　　　　　　　　F#

Chorus:
G#m
　　I hold my breath and close my eyes and
　　　　　　　　　　　　B

G#m
　　dream about her
　　　　　　F#

E　　　　　　　　　　F#　　　　　　　　B
'Cause she's two thousand light years away.

G#m　　　　　　　　B
She hold my malakite so tight,

　　G#m　　　　F#
so never let go,

　　　　　　　　　　　　　　　　w/Riff A 4 times
E　　　　　　　　　F#　　　　　　　B   G#m F#
'Cause she's two thousand light years away,

　　　　　B   G#m F# B G#m F# B G#m F#
years away.

Verse 2:
　　B　　F#
I sit outside and watch the sunrise,

B
　　Look out as far as I can.
　　　　　　　　　　　F#

　　B　　　F#
I can't see her, but, in the distance,

B
　　I hear some laughter, we laugh together.
　　　　　　　　　　　　F#

Chorus:
G#m   B
I hold my breath and close my eyes and

G#m   F#
dream about her

E   F#   B
'Cause she's two thousand light years away.

G#m   B
She hold my malakite so tight,

  G#m   F#
so never let go,

                ***w/Riff A** 4 times*
E   F#   B G#m F#
'Cause she's two thousand light years away,

     B G#m F# B G#m F# B G#m F#
years away.

w/Riff A, 4 times

Interlude: | B G#m | F# | B G#m | F# | B G#m | F# | B G#m | F# ||

     B F#   B   F#
Verse 3: I sit alone in my bedroom staring at the walls.

   B   F#
I've been up all damn night long.

B   F#
My pulse is speeding. My love is yearning.

Chorus:
G#m   B
I hold my breath and close my eyes and

G#m   F#
dream about her

E   F#   B
'Cause she's two thousand light years away.

G#m   B
She hold my malakite so tight,

  G#m   F#
so never let go,

                ***w/Riff A** 4 times*
E   F#   B G#m F#
'Cause she's two thousand light years away,

     B G#m F# B G#m F# B G#m F# | B
years away.   ‖

ALL BY MYSELF

Lyrics by BILLIE JOE
Music by GREEN DAY

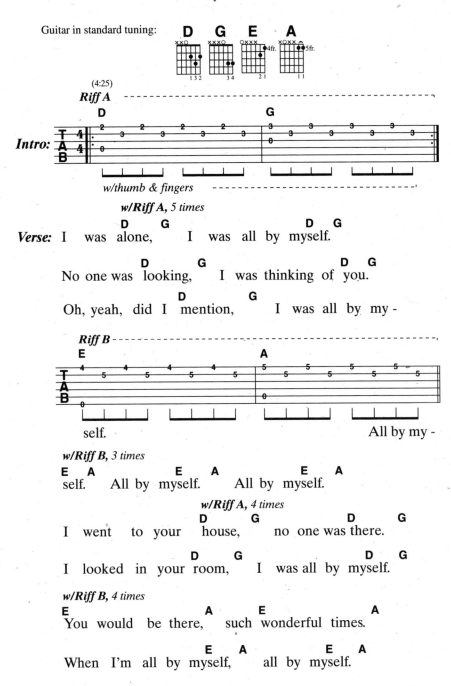

Verse: I was alone, I was all by myself.

No one was looking, I was thinking of you.

Oh, yeah, did I mention, I was all by my -

self. All by my -

self. All by myself. All by myself.

I went to your house, no one was there.

I looked in your room, I was all by myself.

You would be there, such wonderful times.

When I'm all by myself, all by myself.

AMERICAN IDIOT

Words by BILLIE JOE
Music by GREEN DAY

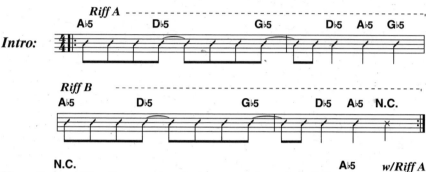

Intro:

Riff A
A♭5 D♭5 G♭5 D♭5 A♭5 G♭5

Riff B
A♭5 D♭5 G♭5 D♭5 A♭5 N.C.

Verse 1:

N.C.   A♭5   *w/Riff A*
Don't want to be an American idiot.

N.C.   A♭5   *w/Riff B*
Don't want a nation under the new media.

N.C.   A♭5   *w/Riff A*
Hey, can you hear the sound of hysteria?

N.C.   A♭5   *w/Riff B*
The subliminal mind - f**k, America.

Chorus:

D♭5
Welcome to a new kind of tension

A♭5
All across the alienation

E♭5   A♭5
Where ev'rything isn't meant to be okay.

D♭5
Television dreams of tomorrow,

A♭5
We're not the ones who're meant to follow,

E♭5
For that's enough to argue.

| N.C. | | A♭5   *w/Riffs A & B* | ‖

Verse 2: N.C.   A♭5   *w/Riff A*
Well, maybe I'm the f**got America.

N.C.   A♭5   *w/Riff B*
I'm not a part of a redneck agenda.

N.C.   A♭5   *w/Riff A*
Now, ev'rybody, do the propaganda,

N.C.   A♭5   *w/Riff B*
And sing along to the age of paranoia.

Chorus: D♭5
Welcome to a new kind of tension

A♭5
All across the alienation

E♭5   A♭5
Where ev'rything isn't meant to be okay.

D♭5
Television dreams of tomorrow,

A♭5
We're not the ones who're meant to follow,

E♭5
For that's enough to argue.

| N.C. | | | A♭5   *w/Riffs A & B 2 times* ‖

Guitar Solo: ‖: D♭5 | A♭5 | E♭5 |【1. A♭5 |:‖【2. A♭5   *w/Riffs A & B* ‖

Verse 3: A♭5 *w/Riff B 3 times*
Don't want to be an American idiot,

One nation controlled by the media.

Information age of hysteria

N.C.
Is calling out to idiot America.

D♭5

Chorus: Welcome to a new kind of tension

A♭5

All across the alienation

E♭5   **A♭5**

Where ev'rything isn't meant to be okay.

D♭5

Television dreams of tomorrow,

A♭5

We're not the ones who're meant to follow,

E♭5

For that's enough to argue.

Outro:

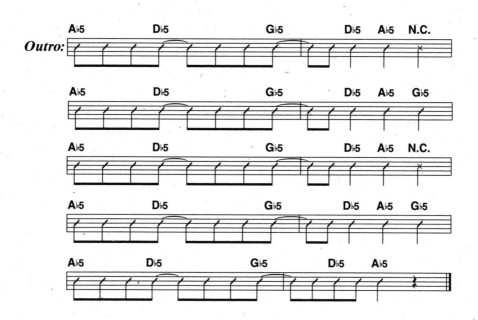

AMERICAN EULOGY

Lyrics by BILLIE JOE
Music by GREEN DAY

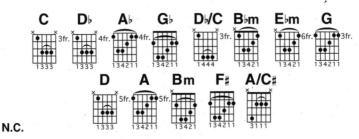

N.C.

Intro: Sing us the song of the century,

it sings like American eulogy.

The dawn of my love and conspiracy

of forgotten hope and the class of thirteen.

Tell me a story into that good night,

sing us a song for me.

A. MASS HYSTERIA

          C Db Ab   **C Db Ab**
Chorus: Hysteria.   Mass   hysteria.

              C Db Ab   **C Db Ab**
  Mass   hysteria.   Mass   hysteria.

     Db   **Ab**
Verse 1:   Red   alert is the color   of panic,

     Db   **Gb**
      elevated to the point   of static.

     Db   **Ab**
      Beating into the hearts of the fanatics and the

     Gb   **Ab**
      neighborhood's a loaded gun.

     Db   **Ab**
      Idle   thought leads to full-throttle screaming,

     Db   **Gb**
      and the welfare's asphyxiating.

D♭   **A♭**
Mass   confusion is all the new rage,   and that's

G♭   **A♭**
creating a feeding ground for the bottom   feeders.

Chorus: **C D♭ A♭**   **C D♭ A♭**
              Hysteria.   Mass   hysteria.

           C D♭ A♭   **C D♭ A♭**
Mass   hysteria.   Mass   hysteria.

Verse 2: **D♭**   **A♭**
          True sounds of maniacal laughter,

      D♭   **G♭**
     and   the   deaf - mute's misleading the   choir,

      D♭   **A♭**
     The   punch - line   is a natural disaster and it's

G♭   **A♭**
sung   by the unemployed.

      D♭   **A♭**
     Fight fire   with   a   riot,

      D♭   **G♭**
     the   class   war   is hanging on a   wire.

      D♭   **A♭**
     Because the martyr is a compulsive   liar when   he

G♭   **A♭**
said, "It's just a bunch of niggers throwing gas into the..."

Chorus: **C D♭ A♭**   **C D♭ A♭**
             Hysteria.   Mass   hysteria.

           C D♭ A♭   **C D♭ A♭**
Mass   hysteria.   Mass   hysteria.

Bridge: **D♭**   **D♭/C**
         There's a disturbance   on the oceanside,

       B♭m   **A♭**
they tapped into the reserve.

      G♭   **E♭m**   **A♭**
     The   static response is so unclear now.

      D♭   **D♭/C**
     Mayday, this is   not a   test!

Bbm
As the neighborhood **Ab** burns,

Gb   **Ebm**   **G** **Ab**
America is falling.

                                G **Ab**
Vigilantes warning ya,   Calling Christian and Gloria!

Interlude:

B. MODERN WORLD

Chorus:
D   **A**   **G**   **A**
I don't   want   to live in the modern world,

D   **A**   **G**   **A**
I don't   want   to live in the modern world.

D   **A**   **G**   **A**
I don't   want   to live in the modern world,

D   **A**   **G**   **A**
I don't   want   to live in the modern world.

Verse 1: Well, I'm the **D** class of thirteen in **A** the era of **G** dissent. **D**

                        A   **G**   **A**
A hostage of the soul   on a strike   to pay the rent.

The   **D** last of the **A** rebels   without a **G** common ground. **D**

                        A   **G**   **A**   **D**
I'm gonna light a fire into the underground. Well,

Chorus:
D ... A ... G ... A
I don't want to live in the modern world,

D ... A ... G ... A
I don't want to live in the modern world.

D ... A ... G ... A
I don't want to live in the modern world,

D ... A ... G ... A
I don't want to live in the modern world.

Bridge:
Bm ... F# ... G ... D ... A/C#
I am a nation without bureaucratic ties.

Bm ... F# ... G ... A
Deny the allegation as it's written, f***ing lies.

Guitar Solo:
‖: D ... A ‖ G ... A :‖ G ... A ... D ‖
| 1.2.3. | 4.

Verse 2:
D ... A ... G ... D
Well, I want to take a ride to the great divide,

A ... G ... A
Beyond the "up to date" and the neo-gentrified.

D ... A ... G ... D
The high definition for the low resident

A ... G ... A ... D
Where the value of your mind is not held in contempt.

Verse 3:
D ... A ... G ... D
I can hear the sound of a beating heart

A ... G ... A
that bleeds beyond a system that is falling apart.

D ... A ... G ... D
With money to burn on a minimum wage,

N.C.
Well, I don't give a shit about the modern age. Yeah!

Chorus:
D ... A ... G ... A
I don't want to live in the modern world,
D ... A ... G ... A
I don't want to live in the modern world.

D ... A ... G ... A
I don't want to live in the modern world,

Repeat chorus and fade

D ... A ... G ... A
I don't want to live in the modern world.

ARE WE THE WAITING

Words by BILLIE JOE
Music by GREEN DAY

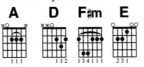

Intro:

Verse 1:

A   D
Starry nights, city of lights coming down over me.

A   D
Skyscrapers, and stargazers in my head.

A   D
Are we, we are, are we, we are the waiting unknown?

F#m   E   D
This dirty town, was burning down in my dreams.

F#m   E   D
Lost and found, city bound in my dreams. And screaming...

Chorus:

A   D
"Are we, we are, are we, we are the waiting?" And screaming...

A   D
"Are we, we are, are we, we are the waiting?"

Verse 2:

A   D
Forget - me - nots, and second thoughts live in isolation.

A   D
Heads or tails, and fairy tales in my mind.

A   D
Are we, we are, are we, we are the waiting unknown?

  F#m   E   D
The rage and love, the story of my life.

  F#m   E   D
The Jesus of Suburbia is a lie. And screaming...

Chorus:

A   D
"Are we, we are, are we, we are the waiting?" And screaming...

Repeat chorus 2 1/2 times

A   D
"Are we, we are, are we, we are the waiting?"

BEFORE THE LOBOTOMY

Lyrics by BILLIE JOE ARMSTRONG
Music by GREEN DAY

To match recording,
tune down 1/2 step:
⑥ = E♭ ③ = G♭
⑤ = A♭ ② = B♭
④ = D♭ ① = E♭

G   D(9)/F♯ Dm(9)/F C   E♭   D5   G5   A5

D   A   E♭ type II   B♭   Cm

Riff A

Intro:

end Riff A

w/Riff A, 2 times

Verse 1:
G   D(9)/F♯
Dreaming, I was only dreaming

Dm(9)/F   C   E♭
of another place and time, where my fam'ly's from.

G   D(9)/F♯
Singing, I can hear them singing,

Dm(9)/F   C   E♭
when the rain had washed away all these scattered dreams.

w/Riff A, 2 times

Verse 2:
G   D(9)/F♯
Dying, ev'ryone's reminded.

Dm(9)/F   C   E♭
Hearts are washed in misery, drenched in gasoline.

G   D(9)/F♯
Laughter, there is no more laughter.

Dm(9)/F   C   E♭
Songs of yesterday now live in the underground.

Play 3 times

Interlude: ‖: D5 G5 A5   D5 | G5 A5 | D5 G5 A5   D5 | G5 A5   :‖

Verse 3:

D   A   G   D   D5 G5 A5 G5 A5 D5
Life   before   the lobotomy.

D   A   G D   D5 G5 A5 G5 A5 D5
Christian sang the eulogy.

D   A   G   D D5 G5 A5 G5 A5 D5
Sign   my love a lost memory,

D   A   G   D D5 G5 A5 G5 A5 D5
From the end of the century.

    G5 D5 A5   G5   D5 A5
Well, it's enough to make you sick,

    G5   D5 A5   G5   D5 A5
To cast a stone and throw a brick.

    G5   D5 A5   G5 D5 A5
But when the sky is falling down,

    G5   D5   A5   G5 D5 A5
It burned your dreams into the ground.

Verse 4:

D   A   G   D D5 G5 A5 G5 A5 D5
Christian's lesson's what he's been sold.

D   A   G   D   D5 G5 A5 G5 A5 D5
We are normal and self-controlled.

D   A   G   D   D5 G5 A5 G5 A5 D5
Remember to learn   to forget,

D   (A)   (G)   (D)   D5 G5 A5 G5 A5 D5
Whiskey shots and cheap cigarettes.

     G5 D5 A5   G5 D5   A5
Well, I'm not stoned, I'm just f***ed up.

  G5 D5 A5   G5   D5   A5
I got so high, I   can't   stand up.

    G5 D5 A5   G5 D5   A5
Well, I'm not cursed, 'cause I've been blessed.

    G5 D5 A5   G5 D5 A5
I'm not in love, 'cause I'm a mess.

Bridge:

      D A   D   A
Like   refugees, we're lost like refugees.

      D. A   D   A
Like   refugees, we're lost like refugees.

      C G   E♭ B♭   D
                type II
The brutality of reality is the freedom that keeps me from...

Interlude:

w/Riff A, 2 times

G   **D(9)/F♯**
Verse 5: Dreaming, I was only dreaming

Dm(9)/F   **C**   **E♭**
  of another place and time, where my fam'ly's from.

G   **D(9)/F♯**
  Singing, I can hear them singing,

Dm(9)/F   **C**   **E♭**
  when the rain had washed away all these scattered dreams.

w/Riff A, 2 times

G   **D(9)/F♯**
Verse 6: Dying, ev'ryone's reminded.

Dm(9)/F   **C**   **E♭**
  Hearts are washed in misery, drenched in gasoline.

G   **D(9)/F♯**
  Laughter, there is no more laughter.

Dm(9)/F   **C**   **Cm**
  Songs of yesterday now live in the underground.

AT THE LIBRARY

Lyrics by BILLIE JOE
Music by GREEN DAY

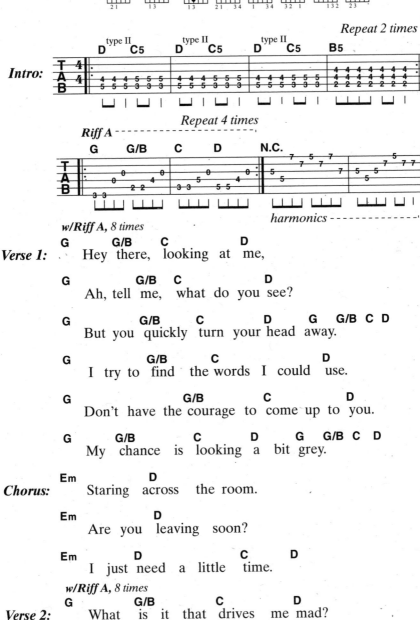

Verse 1:

    w/Riff A, *8 times*

G   G/B   C   D
Hey there, looking at me,

G   G/B C   D
Ah, tell me, what do you see?

G   G/B   C   D   G G/B C D
But you quickly turn your head away.

G   G/B   C   D
I try to find the words I could use.

G   G/B   C   D
Don't have the courage to come up to you.

G   G/B   C   D   G G/B C D
My chance is looking a bit grey.

Chorus:

Em   D
Staring across the room.

Em   D
Are you leaving soon?

Em   D   C   D
I just need a little time.

Verse 2:

    w/Riff A, *8 times*

G   G/B   C   D
What is it that drives me mad?

```
G            G/B       C          D
   Girls  like  you that  I  never   had.
```

```
G          G/B    C              D  G      G/B C  D
   What  is  it  about  you that  I  adore?
```

```
G          G/B       C              D
   What   makes  me  feel  so  much   pain?
```

```
G                   G/B  C        D
   What   makes  me   go  so  insane?
```

```
G            G/B       C          D  G      G/B  C  D
   What   is  it   about you that  I   adore?
```

Chorus:
```
    Em         D
   Staring  across   the room.
```

```
   Em         D
   Are  you  leaving   soon?
```

```
   Em          D           C              D
    I  just  need  a  little  time.  (What time?  Wow!)
```

Interlude:
```
     G            G/B        C                    D    Repeat 8 times
```

Bridge:
```
   G
   Why  did  you  have  to  leave  so  soon?
```

```
                                       D
   Why   did you  have  to  walk  away?
```

w/Riff A, 8 times

Verse 3:
```
   G     G/B      C          D
   Oh,  well,  it  happened  again.
```

```
   G                G/B  C          D
      She walked  away   with  her boyfriend.
```

```
   G       G/B        C       D        G   G/B  C   D
   Maybe  we'll   meet   again  someday.
```

```
   G       G/B      C      D        G   G/B  C   D
   Maybe we'll   meet   again  someday.
```

```
   G       G/B        C       D        G   G/B    C   D
   Maybe  we'll   meet   again  someday.   Someday.
```

Outro:

harmonics - - -

BASKET CASE

Lyrics by BILLIE JOE
Music by GREEN DAY

To match recording,
tune down 1/2 step:
⑥ = E♭   ③ = G♭
⑤ = A♭   ② = B♭
④ = D♭   ① = E♭

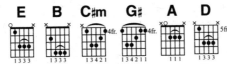

Verse 1:

$\frac{4}{4}$

E
Do you have the time to listen to me whine
                    B   C♯m   G♯

A   E   B
About nothing and ev'rything all at once?

E   B   C♯m   G♯
I am one of those melodramatic fools;

A   E   B
Neurotic to the bone, no doubt about it.

Chorus:

A   B   E
Sometimes I give myself the creeps.

A   B   E
Sometimes my mind plays tricks on me.

A   B   E   D   C♯m
It all keeps adding up. I think I'm cracking up.

A   B   E
Am I just paranoid? Am I just stoned?

Interlude:

E B   C♯m   B   E B   C♯m   B

Verse 2:

E   B   C♯m   G♯
I went to a shrink to analyze my dreams.

A   E   B
She says it's lack of sex that's bringing me down.

E   B   C♯m   G♯
I went to a whore, He said my life's a bore.

A   E   B
So quit whining 'cause it's bringing her down.

Chorus:

A   B   E
Sometimes I give myself the creeps.

A   B   E
Sometimes my mind plays tricks on me.

      A   B   E   D   C#m
It all keeps adding up. I   think   I'm cracking up.

      A   B   E
Am I just paranoid?   Yeah, yeah, yeah.

Interlude:

Bridge: Grasping to control   so I better hold on.

Instrumental:

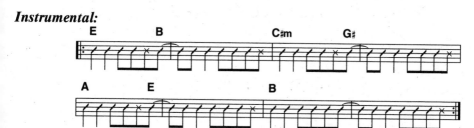

Chorus: Sometimes I give myself the creeps.

      Sometimes my mind plays tricks on me.

It all keeps adding up. I think   I'm cracking up.

Am I just paranoid? Am I just stoned?

Outro:

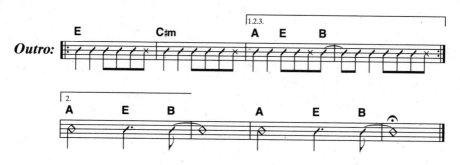

BOULEVARD OF BROKEN DREAMS

Words by BILLIE JOE
Music by GREEN DAY

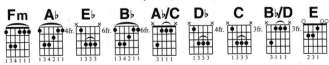

Fm   Ab   Eb   Bb   Ab/C   Db   C   Bb/D   E

Intro:
     Fm   Ab   Eb   Bb

Verse 1:

  Fm   **Ab**
I walk a lonely road,

    Eb   **Bb**   **Fm**
the only one that I have ever known.

          Ab
Don't know where it goes,

  Eb   **Bb**   **Fm**   **Ab Eb Bb**
but it's home to me and I walk alone.

  Fm   **Ab**
I walk this empty street

  Eb   **Bb**   **Fm**
on the boulevard of broken dreams,

        Ab
Where the city sleeps

  Eb   **Bb**   **Fm** **Ab**
and I'm the only one and I walk alone.

 Eb   **Bb**   **Fm** **Ab**
I walk alone, I walk alone.

 Eb   **Bb**   **Ab/C**
I walk alone, I walk a...

Chorus:

 Db **Ab**   **Eb**   **Fm**
My shadow's the only one that walks beside me.

 Db **Ab**   **Eb**   **Fm**
My shallow heart's the only thing that's beating.

 Db   **Ab**   **Eb**   **Fm**
Sometimes I wish someone out there will find me.

 Db   **Ab**   **C**
'Til then I walk alone.

Fm   **A♭**   **E♭**   **B♭**
Ah. Ah. Ah. Ah. Ah.

Fm   **A♭**   **E♭**   **B♭**
Ah. Ah. Ah.

Verse 2: **Fm**   **A♭**
I'm walking down   the line

E♭   **B♭**   **Fm**
that divides me somewhere in my mind.

      A♭   **E♭**
On the borderline of the edge and

B♭   **Fm** **A♭ E♭ B♭**
where I walk alone.

Fm   **A♭**
Read between the lines

E♭   **B♭**   **Fm**
of what's f***ed up and everything's alright.

      A♭
Check my vital signs and

E♭   **B♭**   **Fm** **A♭**
know I'm still alive and I walk alone.

E♭   **B♭**   **Fm** **A♭**
I walk alone, I walk alone.

E♭   **B♭**   **A♭/C**
I walk alone, I walk a...

Chorus: **D♭** **A♭**   **E♭**   **Fm**
My shadow's the only one that walks beside me.

D♭ **A♭** **E♭**   **Fm**
My shallow heart's the only thing that's beating.

D♭ **A♭** **E♭**   **Fm**
Sometimes I wish someone out there will find me.

D♭ **A♭** **C**
'Til then I walk alone.

Fm **A♭** **E♭** **B♭**
Ah. Ah. Ah. Ah. Ah.

Fm **A♭** **E♭**   **B♭**   **A♭/C**
Ah. Ah. I walk alone, I walk a...

40

Guitar
Solo: ‖: D♭   A♭ |¯1.2.3.⌐ E♭   Fm   :‖¯4.⌐ C | ‖

Verse 3:

     Fm   **A♭**
    I walk   this   empty street

    E♭   **B♭**   **Fm**
  on the boulevard of broken dreams,

           A♭
  Where   the city sleeps

     E♭   **B♭**   **A♭/C**
  and I'm the only one and I walk a...

Chorus:

    D♭   **A♭**   **E♭**   **Fm**
  My shadow's the only one that walks beside me.

    D♭   **A♭** **E♭**   **Fm**
  My shallow heart's the only thing that's beating.

    D♭   **A♭**   **E♭**   **Fm**
  Sometimes I wish someone out there will   find   me.

    D♭   **A♭**   **C**
  'Til then I walk alone. | ‖

Outro:

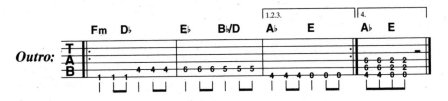

COMING CLEAN

Lyrics by BILLIE JOE
Music by GREEN DAY

To match recording,
tune down 1/2 step:
⑥ = E♭ ③ = G♭
⑤ = A♭ ② = B♭
④ = D♭ ① = E♭

B G#m F# E

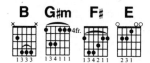

1333 134111 134211 231

Verse 1:
B
Seventeen and strung out on confusion. **G#m**

B
Trapped inside a roll of disillusion. **G#m**

F#
I found out what it takes to be a man. **E**

F#
Now, Mom and Dad will never understand. **E**

Verse 2:
B
Secrets collecting dust but never forget. **G#m**

B
Skeletons come to life in my closet. **G#m**

F#
I found out what it takes to be a man. **E**

F#
Now, Mom and Dad will never understand **E**

What's happening to...

Instrumental Verse:

| **4/4 B** me. | | **G#m** | | **B** | | **G#m** | | |

| **F#** | | **E** | | **F#** | | **E** | | |

Verse 3:
B
Seventeen and coming clean for the first time. **G#m**

B
I finally figured out myself for the first time. **G#m**

F#
I found out what it takes to be a man. **E**

F#
Now, Mom and Dad will never understand **E**

B
What's happening to me.

BRAIN STEW

Lyrics by BILLIE JOE
Music by GREEN DAY

To match recording,
tune down 1/2 step:
⑥ = Eb   ③ = Gb
⑤ = Ab   ② = Bb
④ = Db   ① = Eb

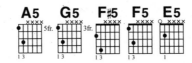

Intro:

Riff A
A5   G5   F#5   F5   E5

Verse 1:

A5   G5   F#5   F5 E5
I'm having trouble trying to sleep.

A5   G5   F#5   F5 E5
I'm counting sheep but running out.

A5   G5   F#5   F5 E5
As time ticks by (and) still I try.

A5   G5   F#5
No rest for crosstops in my mind.

F5   E5
On my own. Here we go.

w/Riff A
‖: A5   G5   F#5   F5   E5   :‖

Verse 2:

A5   G5   F#5   F5 E5
My eyes feel like they're going to bleed,

A5   G5   F#5   F5 E5
Dried up and bulging out my skull.

A5   G5   F#5   F5   E5
My mouth is dry, My face is numb.

A5   G5   F#5
F***ed up and spun out in my room.

F5   E5
On my own. Here we go.

w/Riff A
‖: A5   G5   F#5   F5   E5   :‖

Verse 3:
   A5   **G5**   **F#5** **F5 E5**
My mind is set on overdrive.

   A5   **G5**   **F#5**   **F5 E5**
The clock . is laughing in my face.

   A5   **G5**   **F#5**   **F5**   **E5**
A crooked spine,   My sense is dulled.

   A5   **G5**   **F#5**
Passed the point of delirium.

F5   **E5**
On my own.   Here we go.

w/Riff A

‖:**A5**   **G5**   **F#5**   **F5**   **E5**   :‖

Verse 4:
   A5   **G5**   **F#5** **F5 E5**
My eyes feel like they're going to bleed,

   A5   **G5**   **F#5**   **F5 E5**
Dried   up and bulging out my skull.

   A5   **G5** **F#5**   **F5**   **E5**
My mouth is dry,   My face is numb.

   A5   **G5**   **F#5**
F***ed up and spun out in my room.

F5   **E5**
On my own.   Here we go.

Outro:

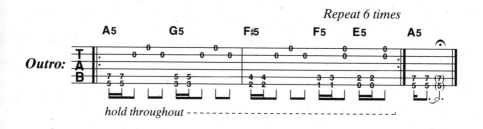

Repeat 6 times

hold throughout -

BURNOUT

Lyrics by BILLIE JOE
Music by GREEN DAY

To match recording,
tune down 1/2 step:
⑥ = E♭   ③ = G♭
⑤ = A♭   ② = B♭
④ = D♭   ① = E♭

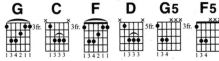

G   C   F   D   G5   F5

Verse 1:

G
I declare I don't
C
care   no more.

G
I'm burning up and out and
C   F   G
growing bored

F
In my smoked out boring
D
room.

G
My hair is shagging in
C
my eyes.

G
Dragging my feet to
C   F   G
hit the street   tonight

F
To drive along these
D
s*** town   lights.

Chorus:

C
I'm not growing up, I'm just
G   C F G
burning out

C
And I stepped in line to
F
walk amongst the
D
dead.

Verse 2:

G
Oh. Apathy has
C
rained on me.

G
And now, I'm feeling
C   F   G
like a soggy dream.

F
So close to drowning, but I
D
don't mind.

G
I've lived inside this
C
mental cave.

G
Throw my emotions
C   F   G
in the grave.

F
Hell, who needs them
D
anyway?

Chorus:

    C   G   C   F   G
I'm not growing up, I'm just burning out

          C   F   D
And I stepped in line to walk amongst the dead.

    C   G   C   F   G
I'm not growing up, I'm just burning out

          C   F   D
And I stepped in line to walk amongst the dead.

| D | | | | | | ‖

Dead.

Interlude:

    C   G   C   F   G
Chorus: I'm not growing up, I'm just burning out

          C   F   D
And I stepped in line to walk amongst the dead.

    C   G   C   F   G
I'm not growing up, I'm just burning out

          C   F   D
And I stepped in line to walk amongst the dead.

| D | | | | | G5 F5 G5 ‖

Dead.

CHRISTIE ROAD

Lyrics by BILLIE JOE
Music by GREEN DAY

To match recording,
tune down 1/2 step:
⑥ = E♭   ③ = G♭
⑤ = A♭   ② = B♭
④ = D♭   ① = E♭

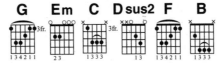

G   Em   C   D sus2   F   B

Verse 1:

G
Staring out of my window,

Em
Watching the cars go rolling by.

C   **D sus2**
My friends are gone, I've got nothing to do.

G
So I sit here patiently,

Em
watching the clock tick so slowly.

C   **D sus2**
Gotta get away, or my brains will explode.

Chorus:
C   **G**   **D sus2**
Give me something to do to kill some time.

C   **G**   **D sus2**
Take me to that place that I call home.

C   **G**   **D sus2**
Take away the strains of being lonely.

C   **G**   **D sus2**
Take me to the tracks at Christie Road.

Verse 2:

G
See the hills from afar

Em
Standing on my beat-up car.

C   **D sus2**
The sun went down and the night fills the sky;

G
Now I feel like me once again;

Em
As the train comes rolling in;

C   **D sus2**
Smoked my boredom gone, slapped my brakes up so high.

Chorus:

C   G   D sus2
Give me something to do to kill some time.

C   G   D sus2
Take me to that place that I call home.

C   G   D sus2
Take away the strains of being lonely.

C   G   D sus2
Take me to the tracks at Christie Road. $\frac{4}{4}$

Interlude:

Riff A - *Repeat 6 times*

G   F   C   F

Bridge:

‖: G   B   F
Mother, stay out of my way,

G   B   F
a - that place we go.

G   B   C
We'll always seem to find our way

                                 Repeat 2 times
G   B   F
to Christie Road.   :‖

           C   F   G
If there's one thing that I need

           C   F   G
that makes me feel complete,

           C   F   G   F   C
So I go to Christie Road, it's home, it's home.

Outro:

w/Riff A, 4 times

G F C F   G   F C F   G   F C F
          It's home,   it's home,

     G   F C F G
it's home.

DOMINATED LOVE SLAVE

Lyrics by BILLIE JOE
Music by GREEN DAY

To match recording,
tune down 1/2 step:
⑥ = Eb ③ = Gb
⑤ = Ab ② = Bb
④ = Db ① = Eb

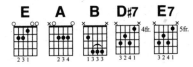

Intro:

Verse 1:
      E   **A**
I want to be your dominated love slave,

E   **B**
Want to be the one who takes the pain.

E   **A**
You can spank me when I do not behave,

E   **B**   **E**
'Mack me in the forehead with a chain.

Chorus:
           A   **E**
'Cause I love feelin' dirty

         B   **E**
and I love feelin' cheap.

         A   **E**
And I love it when you hurt me,

   B   **E**
so drive them staples deep.

Verse 2:
      E   **A**
I want you to slap me and call me naughty.

E   **B**
Put a belt sander against my skin.

E   **A**
Want to feel pain all over my body.

E   **B**   **E**
Can't wait to be punished for my sins.

Chorus: 'Cause I love feelin' dirty
                A   **E**

and I love feelin' cheap.
    B   **E**

And I love it when you hurt me,
       A   **E**

so drive them staples deep.
   B   **E**

Guitar Solo: | E | A | E | B | E | A | E B | E ||

Chorus: 'Cause I love feelin' dirty
                A   **E**

and I love feelin' cheap.
    B   **E**

And I love it when you hurt me,
       A   **E**

so drive... g'night folks.
   B   **D#7 E7**

DON'T LEAVE ME

Lyrics by BILLIE JOE
Music by GREEN DAY

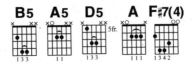

B5 A5 D5 A F♯7(4)

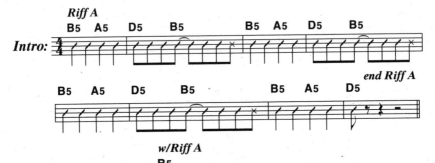

Riff A

B5 A5 D5 B5   B5 A5 D5 B5

Intro:

end Riff A

B5 A5 D5 B5   B5 A5 D5

w/Riff A
B5

Verse 1: I'll go for miles until I find you.

Ah, you say you want to leave me but you can't choose.

w/Riff A, 1st 4 meas. only, 2 times
B5
I've gone through pain ev'ry day and night.

I feel my mind is going insane, something I can't fight.

A　　　　　　**F♯7(4)**
Chorus: Don't leave me.

w/Riff A, meas. 5-8 only
A　　　　　　**F♯7(4)**　　**B5**
Don't leave me.

w/Riff A
B5
Verse 2: A blank expression covering your face.

I'm looking for directions for out of this place.

w/Riff A, 1st 4 meas. only, 2 times
B5
I start to wonder if you'll come back.

I feel the rain storming after thunder I can't hold back.

A　　　　**F♯7(4)**　　**A**　　　　**F♯7(4)**
Chorus: Don't leave me. Don't leave me.

A　　　　**F♯7(4)**　　**A**　　　　**F♯7(4)**
Don't leave me. Don't leave me.

w/Riff A, 1st 4 meas. only, 2 times
B5
Interlude:

Instrumental Chorus:

$\|$: A | | F#7(4) | | A | | F#7(4) | :$\|$

w/Riff A, meas. 5-8 only
B5

w/Riff A
B5
Verse 3: I'll go for miles until I find you.

Ah, you say you want to leave me but you can't choose.

w/Riff A, 1st 4 meas. only, 2 times
B5
I've gone through pain ev'ry day and night.

I feel my mind is going insane, something I can't fight.

A **F#7(4)** **A** **F#7(4)**
Chorus: Don't leave me. Don't leave me.

A **F#7(4)** **A** **F#7(4)**
Don't leave me. Don't leave me.

B5 **A5** **D5** **B5**
Outro:

EAST JESUS NOWHERE

Lyrics by BILLIE JOE
Music by GREEN DAY

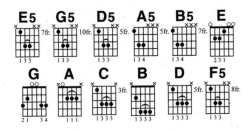

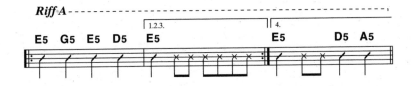

E5
Verse: Raise   your   hands   now to testify.   D5 A5

E5
Your confession will be crucified.   D5 A5

E5
You're   a sacrificial   suicide,   D5 A5

E5
Like   a   dog   that's   been   sodomized.   D5

w/Riff A

A5   E5 G5   E5 D5 E5
Well,   stand   up!   All the white   boys.

E5 G5 E5 D5   E5
Sit   down!   And the black   girls.

E5 G5   E5 D5 E5
Stand   up!   You're the soldiers.

E5 G5 E5 D5   E5   D5 A5
Sit   down!   of the new world.

Pre-chorus:
  B5
Put your   faith   in a miracle   **D5 A5**

  B5
and it's nondenominational. **D5 A5**

  B5
Join   the choir, we'll be singing **D5 A5**

  B5   **D5**
in the church of wishful thinking.

Chorus: **E**   **G**   **A**   **C**   **B**
A fire   burns today of blasphemy and   genocide.

     E   **G**   **A**   **C**   **D**
The sirens of decay will   infiltrate the faith fanatics.

Interlude:

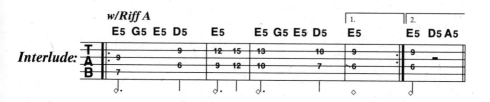

Bridge: **E**   **G**   **B**
Oh, bless me, Lord, for I have sinned.

  E   **G**   **B**
It's been a lifetime since I last confessed.

  E   **G**   **B**
I threw my crutches in the river of a shadow of doubt.

  E   **G**   **B**   **D5 A5**
And I'll be dressed up in my Sunday best.

Pre-chorus:
  B5   **D5 A5**
Say a prayer for the family.

  B5   **D5 A5**
Drop   a coin for humanity.

  B5   **D5 A5**
Ain't this uniform so flattering?

  B5   **D5**
I never asked you a goddamn thing.

Chorus: A fire burns today of blasphemy and genocide.
(E)(G)(A)(C)(B)

The sirens of decay will infiltrate the faith fanatics.
(E)(G)(A)(C)(D)

Interlude: *w/Riff A, 1st 2 meas. only, 4 times*

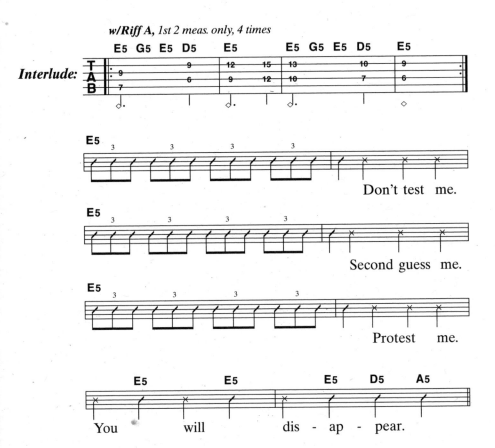

Don't test me.

Second guess me.

Protest me.

You will dis - ap - pear.

Pre-chorus: I want to know who's allowed to breed:
(B5)(D5)(A5)

All the dogs who never learned to read,
(B5)(D5)(A5)

Missionary politicians,
(B5)(D5)(A5)

and the cops of the new religion.
(B5)(D5)

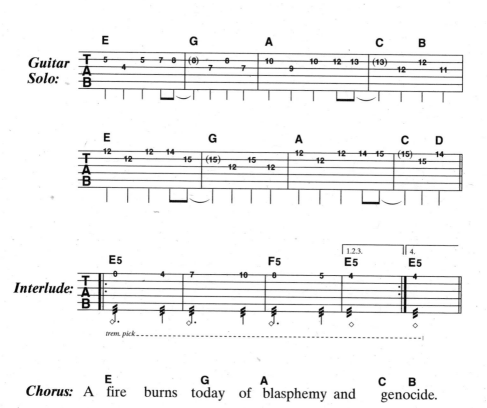

Guitar Solo:

Interlude:

trem. pick

Chorus:

E			G	A			C	B	
A	fire	burns	today	of	blasphemy	and		geno-	cide.

E		G	A		C	B
The	sirens	of decay	will	infiltrate	the	inside.

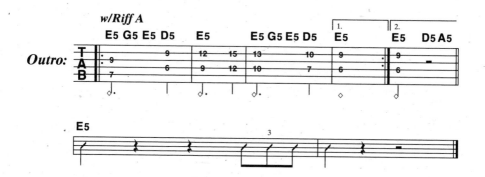

Outro:

EXTRAORDINARY GIRL

Words by BILLIE JOE
Music by GREEN DAY

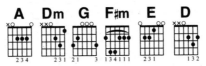

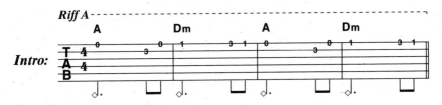

Intro:

Verse 1:

     A   **Dm**   **A**   **Dm**   **A**
She's an extraordinary girl in an ordinary world,

           G   **A**
And she can't seem to get away.

          Dm   **A**   **Dm**
He lacks the courage in his mind, like a child

        A   **G**   **A**
left behind, Like a pet left in the rain.

Chorus:

F#m   **E** **D**   **E**
She's all alone again

F#m   **E**   **D** **E**
wiping the tears from her eyes.

D   **E**
Some days he feels like dying,

D   **Dm**
she gets so sick of crying.

Drums - - - - - - - - , **w/Riff A**

|**N.C.** |**A** |**Dm** |**A** |**Dm**   ‖

Verse 2:

A   **Dm**   **A**   **Dm**
She sees the mirror of herself, an image she wants

    A   **G**   **A**
to sell, To anyone willing to buy.

        Dm   **A**   **Dm**
He steals the image in her kiss, from her hearts

    A   **G**   **A**
apocalypse, From the one called "what's'ername."

Chorus:
F#m   E D   E
She's all alone again

F#m   E   D E
wiping the tears from her eyes.

D   E
Some days he feels like dying,

D   Dm
she gets so sick of crying.

Interlude:

Chorus:
F#m   E D   E
She's all alone again

F#m   E   D E
wiping the tears from her eyes.

D   E
Some days he feels like dying,

D   E
some days it's not worth trying.

D   E
Now that they both are finding

D   Dm   Drums -------,
she gets so sick of crying. |N.C.   ‖

Outro:
A   Dm   A   Dm   A
She's an extraordinary girl, an extraordinary girl,

Dm   A   Dm   A
An extraordinary girl, an extraordinary girl.

F.O.D.

Lyrics by BILLIE JOE
Music by GREEN DAY

To match recording,
tune down 1/2 step:
⑥ = E♭ ③ = G♭
⑤ = A♭ ② = B♭
④ = D♭ ① = E♭

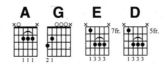

A   G   E   D

        A
Verse 1:   Something's on my mind, it's been for quite some time.

      G   **A**
This time I'm on to you.

So where's the other face? The face I heard before.

       G   **A**
Your head - trip's boring me.

     E   **G**
Pre-chorus: Let's nuke the bridge we torched

      D   **A**
two thousand times before.

  E   **G**   **D**
  This time we'll blast it all to hell.

  E   **G**   **D**   **A**
  I've had this burning in my guts now for so long.

  E   **G**   **D**
  My belly's aching now to say.

      A
Verse 2: Stuck down in a rut of dislogic and smut,

  G   **A**
A side of you well hid.

When it's all said and done, it's real and it's been fun.

     G   **A**
But was it all real fun?

     E   **G**
Pre-chorus: Let's nuke the bridge we torched

      D   **A**
two thousand times before.

E   G   D

This   time   we'll   blast   it   all   to   hell.

E   G   D   A

I've had this   burning   in   my   guts   now   for   so   long.

E   G   D

My   belly's   aching   now   to   say.

Interlude:

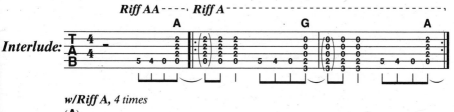

w/Riff A, 4 times
(A)

Chorus: You're   just   a   f***.

I   can't   explain   it   'cause   I   think   you suck.

I'm   taking   pride   in   telling   you to   f*** off and die.

E   G   D   A
Pre-chorus: I've had this   burning   in   my   guts   now   for   so   long.

E   G   D

My   belly's   aching   now   to   say.

E   G   D   A

I'm taking   pleasure   in   the   doubts   I've   passed   to   you.

E   G   D   *w/Riff AA*

So   listen   up   as   you   bite   this.

w/Riff A, 4 times
(A)

Chorus: You're   just   a   f***.

I   can't   explain   it   'cause   I   think   you suck.

I'm   taking   pride   in   telling   you to   f*** off   and   die.

Outro:

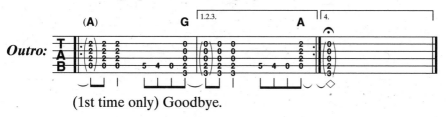

(1st time only) Goodbye.

GEEK STINK BREATH

Lyrics by BILLIE JOE
Music by GREEN DAY

To match recording,
tune down 1/2 step:
⑥ = E♭   ③ = G♭
⑤ = A♭   ② = B♭
④ = D♭   ① = E♭

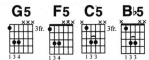

G5   F5   C5   B♭5

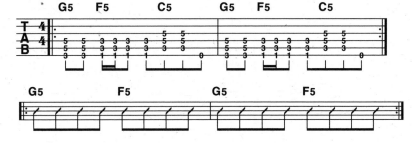

Intro:

       G5   F5   C5   G5   F5   C5

```
T  4 |                        5  5  |                  5  5   |
A  4 | 5  5  3  3  3  3  5  5 |  5  5  5  3  3  3  3  3  5  5  |
B    | 3  3  1  1  1  1     0 |  3  3  1  1  1  1     0        |
```

    G5   F5   G5   F5

Verse 1:

        G5   F5   G5   F5
I'm on a mission, I made my decision,

        G5   F5   G5   F5
lead a path of self - destruction.

        G5   F5   G5   F5
A slow progression, killing my complexion

           G5   F5   G5
and it's rotting out my teeth.

Pre-chorus:

      B♭5   F5   B♭5   F5
I'm on a roll, no self-control,

      B♭5   F5   B♭5   F5
I'm blowing off steam with methamphetamine.

Chorus:

             G5   F5
Well, don't know what I want

           G5   F5
and that's all that I've got,

           G5   F5   G5 | G5 F5 | G5 F5
And I'm picking scabs off my face.

Verse 2:

     G5   F5   G5   F5
Ev'ry hour my blood is turning sour

        G5   F5   G5   F5
And my pulse is beating out of time.

       G5   F5   G5   F5
I found a treasure filled with sick pleasure

           G5   F5   G5
And it sits on a thin white line.

       B♭5   **F5**   **B♭5**   **F5**

Pre-chorus: I'm on a   roll,   no self-control,

         B♭5   **F5**   **B♭5**   **F5**

     I'm   blowing off steam with   methamphetamine.

               G5   **F5**

Chorus: Well, don't know   what   I   want

              G5   **F5**

  and   that's all that I've got,

              G5   **F5**   **G5**

  And I'm   picking scabs off my face.

Repeat 4 times

Interlude:

       G5   **F5**   **C5**   **G5**   **F5**   **C5**

```
T
A
B
   5  5  3 3 3   3  5  5    5  5  3 3 3  3  5  5
   5  5  3 3 3   3  5  5    5  5  3 3 3  3  5  5
   3  3  1 1 1   1     0    3  3  1 1 1  1     0
```

           G5   **F5**   **G5**   **F5**

Verse 3: I'm on a   mission, I   got no decision,

             G5   **F5**   **G5**   **F5**

  Like a   cripple running the rat race.

G5   **F5**   **G5**   **F5**

Wish in one hand and   s*** in the other,

            G5   **F5**   **G5**

  And   see which one gets filled   first.

   B♭5   **F5**   **B♭5**   **F5**

Pre-chorus: I'm on a   roll,   no self-control,

         B♭5   **F5**   **B♭5**   **F5**

     I'm blowing off steam with   methamphetamine.

              G5   **F5**

Chorus: Well,   don't know   what   I   want

              G5   **F5**

  and   that's all that I've got,

              G5   **F5**   **G5**

  And I'm picking scabs off my face.

Repeat 3 times

Outro:

       G5   **F5**   **C5**   **G5**   **F5**   **C5**   **G5**

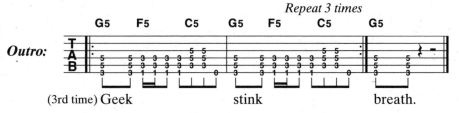

   (3rd time) Geek   stink   breath.

GOING TO PASALACQUA

Lyrics by BILLIE JOE
Music by GREEN DAY

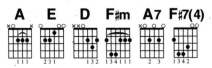

Intro:

Verse 1:
(A)   E   D
Here we go again, infatuation touches me

              A
Just when I thought it would end.

Verse 2:
(A)   E
Oh, but then again it seems much more than that,

    D   A
But I'm not sure exactly what you're thinking.

Pre-chorus:
     D   A
Well, I toss and turn all night

       E
Thinking of your ways of affection

     D   A
But to find that it's not different at all.

     D   A
Well, I throw away my past mistakes

     E
And contemplate my future.

         D
That's when I say, "What the hey."

Chorus:
A   E
Would it last forever?

        F#m   D
Ah, you and I together, hand in hand, we run away.

      A   E
Far away, I'm in for nasty weather.

F♯m
But I'll take whatever you can give

D
That comes my way, yeah. Far away.

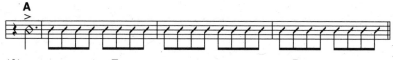

(A)   **E**   **D**
Verse 3:   Here   we go again, infatuation   touches me

                              A
Just when I thought it would end.

(A)   **E**
Verse 4:   Oh, but then   again   it seems   much   more   than   that,

        D   **A**
But I'm not sure exactly what you're thinking.

           D   **A**
Pre-chorus: Well, I   toss and turn all   night

               E
Thinking of   your ways of affection

          D   **A**
But to   find that it's not different at   all.

          D   **A**
Well, I   throw away   my past   mistakes

          E
And   contemplate my future.

               D
That's when   I   say, "What   the hey."

     A   **E**
Chorus: Would it   last forever?

             F♯m   **D**
Ah, you   and I together, hand   in hand,   we run away.

          A   **E**
Far away,   I'm in for nasty   weather.

             F♯m
But I'll take whatever   you can give

             D
That comes my way, yeah. Far away.

Repeat 6 times

Interlude:

Pre-chorus:
           D   **A**
Well, I toss and turn all night

          E
Thinking of your ways of affection

      D   **A**
But to find that it's not different at all.

       D   **A**
Well, I throw away my past mistakes

   E
And contemplate my future.

           D
That's when I say, "What the hey."

Chorus:
   A   **E**
     Would it last forever?

         F#m   **D**
Ah, you and I together, hand in hand, we run away.

        A   **E**
Far away, I'm in for nasty weather.

           F#m
But I'll take whatever you can give

        D
That comes my way, yeah. Far away.

A | **E** | **F#7(4)** | **D** | **A** ||
   Far away.

GREEN DAY

Lyrics by BILLIE JOE
Music by GREEN DAY

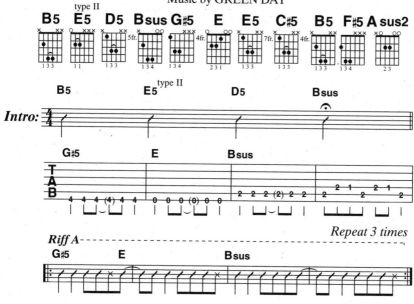

Verse 1:

E5   D5
A small cloud has fallen,

 C#5   B5
the white mist hits the ground.

F#5   A sus2   E
 My lungs comfort me with joy.

E5   D5
Vegging on one detail,

 C#5   B5
the rest just crowds around.

F#5   A sus2   E
 My eyes itch of burning red.

w/Riff A, 4 times

Chorus:

G#5 E   Bsus
 Picture sounds

G#5 E   Bsus
 of moving insects so surreal.

G#5 E   Bsus
 Lay around.

G#5 E   Bsus
 Looks like I found something new.

66

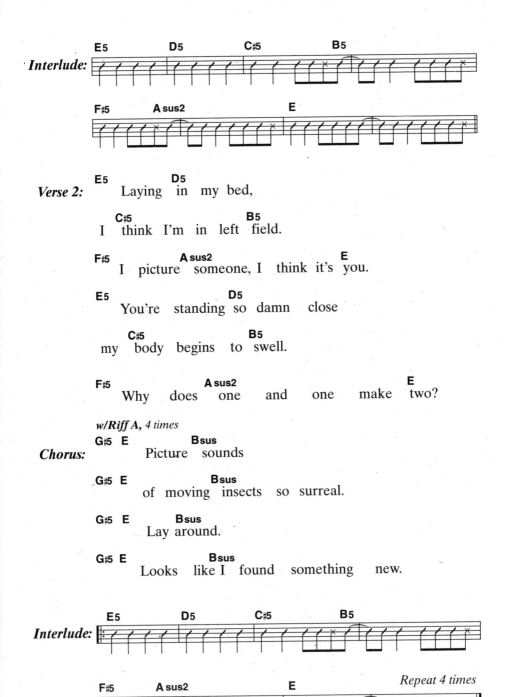

Interlude:

E5   D5   C#5   B5

F#5   A sus2   E

Verse 2:

E5   D5
Laying in my bed,

C#5   B5
I think I'm in left field.

F#5   A sus2   E
I picture someone, I think it's you.

E5   D5
You're standing so damn close

C#5   B5
my body begins to swell.

F#5   A sus2   E
Why does one and one make two?

w/Riff A, 4 times

G#5 E   B sus
Chorus: Picture sounds

G#5 E   B sus
of moving insects so surreal.

G#5 E   B sus
Lay around.

G#5 E   B sus
Looks like I found something new.

Interlude:

E5   D5   C#5   B5

F#5   A sus2   E   *Repeat 4 times*

Verse 3:

E5   D5
Laying in my bed,

    C#5   B5
I think I'm in left field.

F#5   A sus2   E
I picture someone, I think it's you.

E5   D5
You're standing so damn   close

    C#5   B5
my body begins to swell.

F#5   A sus2   E
Why does one and one make two?

w/Riff A, 4 times

Chorus:

G#5 E   Bsus
         Picture sounds

G#5 E   Bsus
    of moving insects so surreal.

G#5 E   Bsus
    Lay around.

G#5 E   Bsus
    Looks like I found something new.

Outro:

E5   D5   C#5   B5   A sus2

GOOD RIDDANCE (TIME OF YOUR LIFE)

Lyrics by BILLIE JOE
Music by BILLIE JOE and GREEN DAY

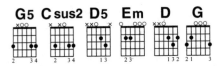

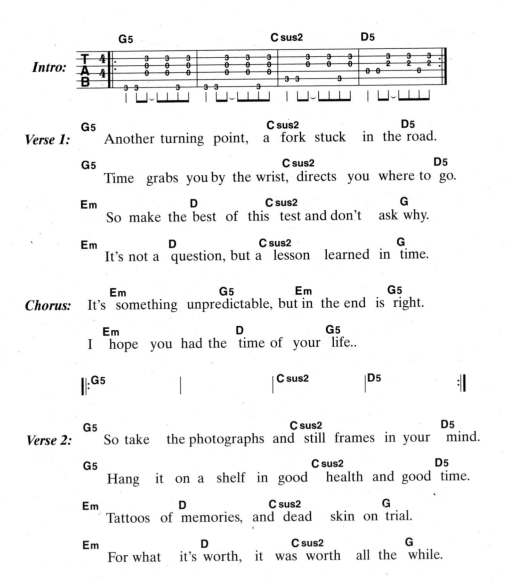

Intro:

Verse 1:

G5
Another turning point, a fork stuck in the road.

G5   C sus2   D5
Time grabs you by the wrist, directs you where to go.

Em   D   C sus2   G
So make the best of this test and don't ask why.

Em   D   C sus2   G
It's not a question, but a lesson learned in time.

Chorus:

Em   G5 Em   G5
It's something unpredictable, but in the end is right.

Em   D   G5
I hope you had the time of your life..

‖: G5 | | C sus2 | D5 | :‖

Verse 2:

G5   C sus2   D5
So take the photographs and still frames in your mind.

G5
Hang it on a shelf in good health and good time.

Em   D   C sus2   G
Tattoos of memories, and dead skin on trial.

Em   D   C sus2   G
For what it's worth, it was worth all the while.

Chorus:
    Em   G5   Em   G5
It's something unpredictable, but in the end is right.

     Em   D   G5
I hope you had the time of your life..

‖: G5 | | C sus2 | D5   :‖

Interlude: | G5 | | C sus2 | D5 | G5 | | C sus2 | D5 |

| Em | D | C sus2 | G | Em | D | C sus2 | G ‖

Chorus:
    Em   G5   Em   G5
It's something unpredictable, but in the end is right.

     Em   D   G5
I hope you had the time of your life..

‖: G5 | | C sus2 | D5   :‖

Chorus:
    Em   G5   Em   G5
It's something unpredictable, but in the end is right.

     Em   D   G5
I hope you had the time of your life..

                               1.   2.
‖: G5 | | C sus2 | D5   :‖ D5 | G5   ‖

THE GROUCH

Lyrics by BILLIE JOE
Music by BILLIE JOE and GREEN DAY

A   E   D   F♯m

Verse 1:
A / E / A / D
I was a young boy that had big plans.

A / E / D / E
Now I'm just another s***ty old man.

A / E / A / D
I don't have fun and I hate ev'rything.

A / E / A
The world owes me, so f*** you.

A / E / A / D
Glory days don't mean s*** to me.

A / E / D E
I drank a six-pack of apathy.

A / E / A / D
Life's a bitch and so am I.

A / E / A
The world owes me, so f*** you.

Chorus:
F♯m / D / A / E
Wasted youth and a fist full of ideals;

F♯m / D / A / E
I had a young and optimistic point of view.

F♯m / D / A / E
Wasted youth and a fist full of ideals;

F♯m / D / A / E
I had a young and optimistic point of view.

Verse 2:
A / E / A / D
I've decomposed, yet, my gut's gettin' fat.

A / E / D / E
Oh my God, I'm turnin' out like my Dad.

A / E / A / D
I'm always rude, I got a bad attitude.

A / E / A
The world owes me, so f*** you.

    A   E   A   D
The   wife's a   nag and the kid's f***ing up.

    A   E   D   E
I   don't   have   sex 'cause I can't   get it up.

    A   E   A   D
I'm just a   grouch sitting on the couch.

         A   E   A
The world   owes   me, so f*** you.

      F#m   D   A   E
Chorus: Wasted youth and a   fist full of ideals;

      F#m   D   A   E
I had a   young and optimistic point   of view.

      F#m   D   A   E
Wasted youth and a   fist full of ideals;

      F#m   D   A   E
I had a   young and optimistic point   of view.

Instrumental Verse:

| A E | A D | A E | D E | A E | A D | A E | A | ‖

Instrumental Chorus:

           Repeat 3 times

‖: F#m   D | A   E   :‖ F#m   D | A | E | ‖

       A   E   A   D
Verse 3: I was   a   young boy   that   had   big   plans.

    A   E   D   E
Now   I'm just another s***ty old man.

    A   E   A   D
I   don't   have   fun and I hate   ev'rything.

       A   E   A
The world   owes   me, so f***you.

    A   E   A   D
Glory   days   don't   mean   s***   to me.

    A   E   D E
I   drank   a   six-pack   of apathy.

    A   E   A   D
Life's   a   bitch   and so am I.

      A   E   A
The world   owes   me, so f***you.

      A   E   A
The world   owes   me, so f***you.

      A   E   D   A
The world   owes   me, so f***you.

HITCHIN' A RIDE

Lyrics by BILLIE JOE
Music by BILLIE JOE and GREEN DAY

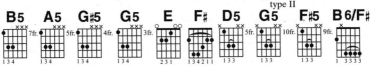

Intro:

| B5 | A5 | G#5 | G5 |

Verse 1:

B5   A5   G#5   G5
Hey,   mister, where you headed?

B5   A5   G#5   G5
Are   you   in a hurry?

B5   A5   G#5   G5   B5 A5 G#5 G5
I need   a lift to happy hour, say, oh no.

B5   A5   G#5   G5
Do you break for distilled spirits?

B5   A5   break   G#5   G5
I need a break   as well.

B5   A5   G#5 G5
The well that inebriates the guilt.

B5   A5   G#5   G5
One,   two.   One, two, three, four.

Repeat 3 times

‖: B5   A5 | G#5   G5 :‖ B5   A5 | G#5   N.C.   ‖

Verse 2:

B5   A5   G#5   G5
Cold   turkey's getting stale,

B5   A5   G#5   G5
tonight I'm eating   crow.

B5   A5   G#5 G5   B5   A5   G#5   G5
Fermented salmonella, poison oak, no.

B5   A5   G#5   G5
There's a drought at the fountain of youth,

B5   A5 G#5   G5
and now I'm dehydrated.

B5   A5   G#5   G5
My tongue is swelling up, I say,

B5   A5   G#5   G5
One,   two.   One, two, three, four.

Repeat 4 times

‖: **B5**   **A5** | **G♯5**   **G5**   :‖

        E   **F♯**   **B5**   **A5**   **G♯5**   **G5**

Chorus: Troubled times, you know I cannot lie.

        E   **F♯**

        I'm off the wagon and I'm hitchin' a ride.

‖: **B5**   **A5** | **G♯5**   **G5**   :‖

        B5   **A5**   **G♯5**   **G5**

Verse 3: There's a drought at the fountain of youth,

        B5   **A5**   **G♯5**   **G5**

        and now I'm dehydrated.

        B5   **A5**   **G♯5**   **G5** | **N.C.** | ‖

        My tongue is swelling up, I say...

                                type II   *Repeat 8 times*

Guitar ‖: **B5**   **D5** | **G5** ^{type II}   **F♯5**   :‖
Solo:

        E   **F♯**   **B5**   **A5**   **G♯5**   **G5**

Chorus: Troubled times, you know I cannot lie.

        E   **F♯**

        I'm off the wagon and I'm hitchin' a ride.

                            type II   *Repeat 7 times*

Outro: ‖: **B5**   **D5** | **G5** ^{type II}   **F♯5**   :‖
          (ride.)   Hitchin'   a

       | **B5**   **A5** | **G♯5**   **N.C.** | **B 6/F♯**   ‖
       (ride.)

HOLIDAY

Words by BILLIE JOE
Music by GREEN DAY

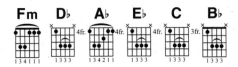

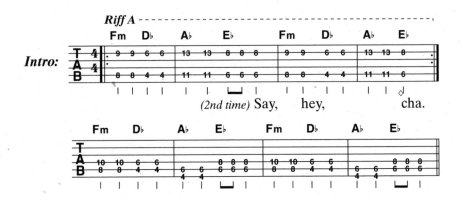

Intro:

(2nd time) Say,   hey,   cha.

Verse 1:

Fm   Db   Ab   Eb
Hear the sound of the falling rain

Fm   Db   Ab   C   Fm
coming down like an Armageddon flame. (Hey.)

Db   Ab   Eb   C
The shame, the ones who died without a   name.

Fm   Db   Ab   Eb
Hear the dogs howling out of key

Fm   Db   Ab   C   Fm
to a hymn   called   "Faith and misery," (Hey)

Db   Ab   Eb   C
And   bleed, the company lost the war today.

Chorus:

Fm   Db   Ab   Eb
I beg to dream and differ from   the hollow lies.

Fm   Db   Ab   C
This is the dawning of the rest of our lives on holiday.

w/Riff A

|Fm   Db |Ab   Eb |Fm   Db |Ab   Eb   ‖

Verse 2:

Fm   Db   Ab Eb
Hear the drum pounding out of time,

Fm   Db Ab C   Fm
another protestor has crossed the line (Hey.)

   Db   Ab   Eb   C
To find the money's on the other side.

Fm   Db Ab   Eb Fm
Can I get another "Amen?" (Amen.)

    Db   Ab   C Fm
There's a flag wrapped around a score of men. (Hey.)

   Db Ab Eb   C
A gag, a plastic bag on a monument.

Chorus:

Fm   Db   Ab   Eb
I beg to dream and differ from the hollow lies.

Fm   Db   Ab   C
This is the dawning of the rest of our lives on holiday.

Interlude:

Hey!

Guitar Solo:
||: Db | Ab | C | Fm Eb :|| C | | | ||
(1. / 2..)

w/Riff B, 2 times

Interlude:
| Fm Ab | Db Bb Eb C | Fm Ab | Eb C Fm |

| Fm Ab | Db Bb Eb C | Fm Ab | Eb C Fm ||

(Spoken:) The representative from California has the floor.

w/Riff B, 4 times

Bridge:
||: Fm Ab | Db Bb Eb C | Fm Ab | Eb C Fm :||

Zieg Heil to the President gasman, bombs away is your punishment.
Pulverize the Eiffel Towers, who criticize your government.
Bang, bang goes the broken glass and kill all the fags that don't agree.
Trials by fire setting fire is not a way that's meant for me. meant for me?

C
Just 'cause... just 'cause, because we're outlaws, yeah.

Chorus:
    Fm   **D♭**   **A♭**   **E♭**
    I beg to dream and differ from the hollow lies.

    Fm   **D♭**   **A♭**   **C**
    This is   the dawning of the rest of our lives.

    Fm   **D♭**   **A♭**   **E♭**
    I beg to dream and differ   from the hollow lies.

    Fm   **D♭**   **A♭**   **C**
    This is the dawning of the rest of our lives...

    this is our lives on holiday.

Outro:

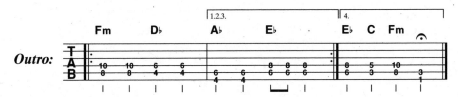

HORSESHOES AND HANDGRENADES

Lyrics by BILLIE JOE
Music by GREEN DAY

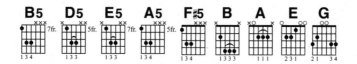

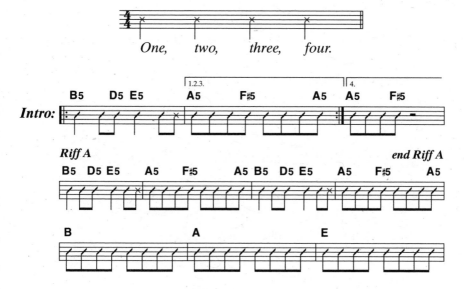

Verse 1:
G I'm not f***ing around. *B5 w/Riff A, 4 times* I think I'm coming out.

All the deceivers and cheaters,

I think we've got a bleeder right now.

Want you to slap me around. Want you to knock me out.

Well, you missed me, kissed me,

Now you better kick me down.

Chorus:

E

       Maybe you're the runner - up,

A   B   A

But the first one to lose the race.

E

       Almost only really counts in

F♯5

Horseshoes and hand grenades.

B5 *w/Riff A, 4 times*

Verse 2: I'm gonna burn it all down. I'm gonna rip it out.

Well, ev'rything that you employ was

meant for me to destroy to the ground now.

So don't f***me around because I'll shoot you down.

I'm gonna drink, fight and f*** and I'm

pushing my luck all the time now.

Chorus:

E

       Maybe you're the runner - up,

A   B   A

But the first one to lose the race.

E

       Almost only really counts in

F♯5

Horseshoes and handgrenades.

B5 A5   **B5 A5**

Bridge 1: Demolition, self destruction,

B5   **A5**   **B5**   **A5**

What to annihilate, This age - old contradiction.

Interlude:

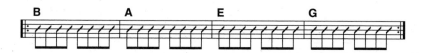

Bridge 2:

B   A
Demolition,   self destruction,

E   G
What   to   annihilate, This age - old contradiction.

B   A
Demolition,   self destruction,

E   G   **B5** *w/Riff A*
What   to   annihilate, this   old age.

                          B5 *w/Riff A, 2 times*
Verse 3:   I'm not f***ing   around.   I   think   I'm coming out.

Well,   I'm a   hater, a   traitor in   a   pair of   Chuck Taylors

right   now.   I'm not f***ing   around.

Outro:

                                 G-L-O-R-I-A!

HOMECOMING

Words by BILLIE JOE
Music by GREEN DAY

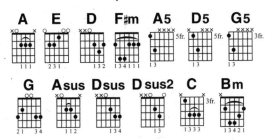

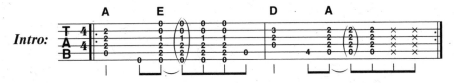

I. THE DEATH OF ST. JIMMY

Verse 1:

A   E   D   A   E   D A
My heart is beating from me, I am standing all alone.

E   D   A   E   D   A
Please call me only if you are coming home.

E   A
Waste another year flies by,

E   A
waste a night or two.

D   A   D   A E
You taught me how to live.

Interlude:

A   D   E   A   D A D   E

Verse 2:

(E)   A   D E
In the streets of shame

A   D   A D E
where you've lost your dreams in the rain.

A   D E
There's no signs of hope,

D   A D E
the stems and seeds of the last of the dope.

Verse 3: (E) There's a A glow D of E light,

the Saint A Jimmy is D the spark A in D the E night.

Bearing A gifts D and E trust,

a fixture D in the city A of D lust. E

Pre-chorus: What the F#m hell's E your A name?

What's your F#m pleasure, what E is your A pain?

Do you F#m dream E too A much?

Do you think D what you need A is a E crutch?

Interlude:

Verse 4: In the crowd A of D pain E

Saint Jimmy A comes without D any A D shame. E

He says we're A f***ed up but we're D not the E same,

and mom and D dad are the ones A you D can blame. E

Pre-chorus: Jimmy F#m died E A today.

He blew his F#m brains out E into A the bay.

In the F#m state E of A mind,

it's my D own private A suicide. E A5

II. EAST 12TH ST.

Riff A

D5 A5 G5 A5   D5 A5 G5 A5

(2nd time) Well,

82

Chorus: (A5)   D5 *w/Riff A, 4 times*

Chorus: Well, nobody cares. Well, nobody cares.

Does anyone care if nobody cares?

Well, nobody cares. Well, nobody cares.

Does anyone care if nobody cares?

Verse:
```
D                    G    D
Jesus  filling  out paperwork now

G           A        Asus  A
at  the facility on East   12th Street.

D            G      D
He's not listening to  a   word   now,

G                      A       Asus  A
he's   in his own world and he's daydreaming.

D                  G         D
He'd   rather be doing  something else, now,

    G                          A      Asus A
like  cigarettes and coffee  with the under  belly.

    D                      G D
His  life's  on the line with  anxiety now,

G                 A        Asus A
she  had  enough and he's had  plenty.
```

Bridge:
```
D Dsus D Dsus2 D                A  G  A  D
                 Somebody get me out of  here.

D Dsus D Dsus2 D                A  G  A  D
                 Anybody get me out of  here.

D Dsus D Dsus2 D                A  G  A  D
                 Somebody get me out of  here.

D Dsus D Dsus2 D              A      G  A  D
                 Get me the f*** right   out of  here.

C                 A
   So  far  away,    I   don't  wanna stay.

C                          A
   Get me out of  here   right  now.
```

   C   **A**

I just want to be free, is there a possibility?

   C   **A**

Get me out of here right now.

C A C A C A C A

Ah. Ah. Ah. Ah. Right!

D C G A D G A D

This life-like dream ain't for me.

III. NOBODY LIKES YOU

D

Verse:

D fell **A** asleep while **G** watching Spike **A** TV

I fell asleep while watching Spike TV

       D   **A**   **G**   **A**

after ten cups of coffee and you're still not here.

D   **A**   **G**   **A**

Dreaming of a song but something went wrong.

         D   **A**   **G**   **A**

And you can't tell anyone 'cus no one's here.

Bm   **A**   **G**   **D**

Left me here alone when I should have stayed home.

      Bm   **A**   **D**   **A**

After ten cups of coffee I'm thinking... (Where'd you go?)

Chorus:

D   **A**   **G**   **A**

Nobody likes you. Ev'ryone left you. (Where'd you go?)

       D   **A**   **G**   **A**

They're all out without you havin' fun. (Where'd you go?)

D   **A**   **G**   **A**

Ev'ryone left you. Nobody likes you. (Where'd you go?)

       D   **A**   **G**   **A**

They're all out without you havin' fun. (Where'd you go?)

IV. ROCK AND ROLL GIRLFRIEND

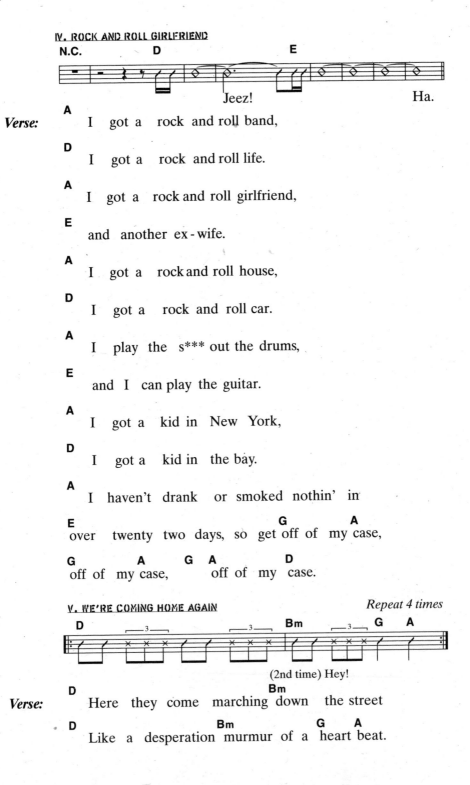

N.C.　　　　D　　　　　　　　　E

Jeez!　　　　　　　　　　　　Ha.

Verse:

A
I got a rock and roll band,

D
I got a rock and roll life.

A
I got a rock and roll girlfriend,

E
and another ex - wife.

A
I got a rock and roll house,

D
I got a rock and roll car.

A
I play the s*** out the drums,

E
and I can play the guitar.

A
I got a kid in New York,

D
I got a kid in the bay.

A
I haven't drank or smoked nothin' in

E　　　　　　　　　　　　　G　　　　A
over twenty two days, so get off of my case,

G　　　　A　　　G　　A　　　　D
off of my case,　off of my case.

V. WE'RE COMING HOME AGAIN　　　　*Repeat 4 times*

D　　　　　　3　　　　　　3　　　Bm　　　3　　G　　A

(2nd time) Hey!

Verse:

D　　　　　　　　　　　　　　　　Bm
Here they come marching down the street

D　　　　　　　　　　Bm　　　　　G　　A
Like a desperation murmur of a heart beat.

D   Bm
Coming back from the edge of town

G   A   G   A
underneath their feet.

D   Bm
The time has come and it's goin' nowhere.

D   Bm   G   A
Nobody ever said that life was fair, now.

D   Bm
Go - karts and guns are treasures they will bare

G   A   D   A
in the summerheat.

G   A
Pre-chorus: The world is spinning around,

G   A   D   A
around out of control again.

G   A   Bm   E
From the Seven Eleven to the fear of breaking down.

D   G   A   D   G   A
So send my love a letter bomb and visit me in hell.

G   A   G A |D | |A | ‖
We're the ones going...

D   Dsus   D   Dsus2   D   A
Chorus: Home,   we're coming home again.

D   Dsus   D   Dsus2   D   A
Home,   we're coming home again.

G
I started f***in' running as soon as my

D
feet touched ground.

G
We're back in the barrio,

       A
and to you and me that's jingle town. That's...

Repeat 4 times
‖: D   A
Home, we're coming home again. :‖

Repeat 4 times
‖: D   A   G
Home, we're coming home again. :‖

D
Outro: Nobody likes you, ev'ryone left you.

They're all out without you having fun.

JADED

Lyrics by BILLIE JOE
Music by GREEN DAY

To match recording,
tune down 1/2 step:
⑥ = E♭ ③ = G♭
⑤ = A♭ ② = B♭
④ = D♭ ① = E♭

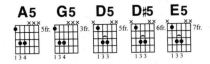

A5 G5 D5 D♯5 E5

Repeat 4 times

Intro:

Riff A

| A5 | | G5 | D5 |

Verse 1:

A5　　　　G5　　　D5　　　A5　　　　　　　G5 D5
Somebody keep my balance, I think I'm falling off

A5　　　G5　　　　D5　A5　G5 D5
into a state of regression.

A5　　　　G5　　D5　　A5　　　　　G5 D5
The expiration date rapidly coming up.

A5　　　　　G5　D5　　　A5
It's leaving me behind to rank.

Chorus:

D5
Always move forward.

　　　　　　　　　　　　　　A5　　　G5 A5　　　G5 A5
Going "straight" will get you nowhere.

D5
There is no progress.

　　　　　　　　　D♯5 E5
Evolution killed it all.

I found my place in nowhere.

w/Riff A, 2 times
|A5 　　　　|G5　　D5　|A5　　　　　|G5　　　D5　‖

Verse 2:

A5　　　　G5　　　D5　　　A5　　　　G5　　　D5
I'm taking one step sideways, leading with my crutch.

A5　　　　　　　　　G5　D5 A5　　G5 D5
Got a f***ed up equilibrium.

A5　　　　　　G5　　D5　　　A5　　　　　　G5 D5
Count down from nine to five. Hooray! We're gonna die,

A5　　　　G5　　D5　A5
Blessed into our extinction.

D5

Chorus: Always move forward.

                                          A5   **G5 A5**   **G5 A5**

Going   "straight" will get you nowhere.

D5

      There   is no progress.

                      D#5 E5

Evolution killed   it all.

I   found   my place in nowhere.

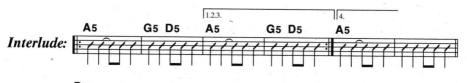

Interlude:

D5

Chorus: Always move   forward.

                                          A5   **G5 A5**   **G5 A5**

Going   "straight" will get you nowhere.

D5

      There   is no progress.

                     D#5 E5

Evolution killed   it all.

I   found   my place in nowhere.

A5 G5 D5   **A5**   **G5 D5**

        In   nowhere.

       A5 G5 D5 A5   **G5 D5 A5**

In no   -   where.

J.A.R. (JASON ANDREW RELVA)

Lyrics by MIKE DIRNT
Music by GREEN DAY

To match recording,
tune down 1/2 step:
⑥ = E♭   ③ = G♭
⑤ = A♭   ② = B♭
④ = D♭   ① = E♭

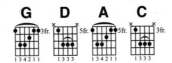

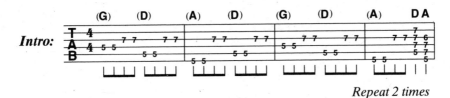

Repeat 2 times

Verse 1:

G   A   G
My friend drove off the other day,

D   A   G   A
And now he's gone and all they say is you gotta live

G D A
'cause life goes on.

G   A   G
But now I see I'm mortal too,

D   A   G
I can't live my life like you,

A   G D A
Gotta live it up while life goes on.

Chorus:

G   D
And I think it's alright

A
That I do what I like,

G   D
'Cause that's the way I wanna live.

A
And so I give, and I'm still

|G D   D |A   D |G   D |A   D A ‖
giving.

         G   A   G

Verse 2:   But now I wonder 'bout   my friend,

            D   A   G

If he gave all he could   give,

                      A   G   D A

'Cause he lived   his life like I live mine.

    G   A   G

    If you could see inside my head,

                     D   A G

Then you'd start to understand

                  A   G   D A

the things I value in my heart.

           G   D

Chorus: And   I think it's alright

                       A

That   I do what I like,

                           G   D

'Cause that's the way I wanna live.

              A

And so I give, and I'm still

| G D | A D | G D | A D | G D | A D | G D | A D ‖

giving.

           C   G   D   A

Bridge: You know that,   I know   that

           C   G   A   D A

    you're watching me.

                                       Repeat 4 times

             G   A   G   D   A

Guitar Solo:

           G   D

Chorus: And   I think   it's alright

                       A

That   I do what I like,

90

                                        G   **D**
'Cause that's the way I wanna live.

                A
And so I give, and I'm still

| G D | A D | G D | A D | G D | A D | G D | A D ||
giving.

Outro: (G)   (D)
Gotta make a plan,

      (A)   (D)
Gotta do what's right,

       (G)   (D)
Can't run around in circles

     (A)   (D)
If you wanna build a life.

         (G)   (D)
But I don't wanna make a plan

      (A)   (D)
For a day far away,

       (G)   (D)
While I'm young and while I'm able

     (A)   (D)
All I wanna do is...

JESUS OF SUBURBIA

Words by BILLIE JOE
Music by GREEN DAY

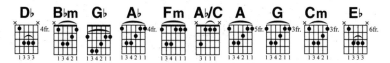

I. JESUS OF SUBURBIA

Verse 1:

D♭
I'm the son of rage and love,

B♭m
the Jesus of Suburbia,

G♭
From the bible of "none of the above,"

A♭
On a steady diet of...

D♭
soda pop and Ritalin.

B♭m
No one ever died from my

G♭
sins in hell as far as I can tell,

A♭
At least the ones I got away with.

Pre-chorus:
        G♭   **A♭**
But there's nothing wrong with me.

        G♭   **A♭**
This is how I'm s'posed to be

      G♭   **A♭**
In a land of make believe

         D♭ A♭ G♭   **D♭ A♭ G♭**
that don't believe in me.

Verse 2:

D♭
Get my television fix,

B♭m
sitting on my crucifix.

G♭
The living room in my private womb,

A♭
While the moms and Brads are away.

D♭
To fall in love and fall in debt

B♭m
to alcohol and cigarettes and

G♭
Mary Jane to keep me insane

A♭
and doing someone else's cocaine.

G♭   **A♭**
Pre-chorus: But there's nothing wrong with me.

G♭   **A♭**
This is how I'm s'posed to be

G♭   **A♭**
In a land of make believe

D♭ A♭ G♭ **D♭ A♭ G♭**
that don't believe in me.

Interlude:

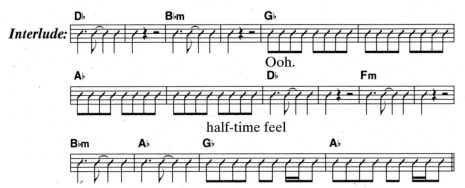

Ooh.

half-time feel

II. CITY OF THE DAMNED

D♭   **A♭/C**
Verse 1: At the center of the earth in the parking lot

B♭m   **A♭**
of the Seven Eleven where I was taught

G♭   **A♭**
the motto was just a lie.

D♭
It says "Home is where your heart is."

A♭/C
But what a shame 'cause

B♭m   **A♭**
ev'ryone's heart doesn't beat the same.

G♭   **A♭**
We're beating out of time.

Chorus:
B♭m   **A♭**
City of the dead

D♭   **G♭**
at the end of another lost highway.

B♭m   **A♭**   **G♭**
Signs misleading to nowhere.

B♭m   **A♭**
City of the damned,

D♭   **G♭**
lost children with dirty faces today.

B♭m   **A♭**   **G♭**
No one really seems to care.

Verse 2:
D♭   **A♭/C**
I read the graffiti in the bathroom stall

B♭m   **A♭**
like the Holy Scriptures of the shopping mall.

G♭   **A♭**
And so it seemed to confess.

D♭   **A♭/C**
It didn't say much but it only confirmed

B♭m   **A♭**
that the center of the earth is the end of the world.

G♭   **A♭**
And I could really care less.

Chorus:
B♭m   **A♭**
City of the dead

D♭   **G♭**
at the end of another lost highway.

B♭m   A♭   G♭

Signs   misleading to nowhere.

B♭m   A♭

City   of the damned,

D♭   G♭

lost children with   dirty faces today.

B♭m   A♭   G♭

No one really seems to care.

Hey!

III. I DON'T CARE

Interlude:

```
          Ab        Db        Ab        Db
T 3                 2  2  2              1
A 4  1  1     1  1           1  1   1  1    4   2
B 4
     V  I  V  I  I  I  I  I  V  I  V  I  I  I  I  I

          Gb        Db        Ab
T    2  2     2  2     1
A               4  2  4  4     4  4         4
B
     V  I  V  I  I  I  I  V  I  V  I     ◇.
```

Chorus: ‖: A♭
       I   don't care D♭ if you don't...

A♭   D♭

I   don't care if you don't...

G♭   D♭   A♭   *Repeat Chorus 4 times*

I   don't care if you don't care.   :‖

G♭ A♭   D♭ A A♭ D♭ A A♭ D♭ A A♭ D♭ A A♭

I   don't   care.

Verse: D♭   A A♭

Ev'ryone's so full of s***,

D♭   A A♭

born and raised by hypocrites.

D♭   A A♭

Hearts recycled but never saved

D♭   A A♭

from   the cradle to the grave.

D♭   A   A♭

We are the kids of war and peace

D♭   A A♭

from Anaheim to the Middle East.

D♭   **A** **A♭**
We are the stories and disciples of

D♭   **A** **A♭**
the Jesus of Suburbia.

Bridge: **G♭**   **A♭** **D♭** **A♭**
Land of make believe,

G♭   **A♭**   **D♭** **A♭**
and it don't believe in me.

G♭   **A♭** **D♭** **A♭**
Land of make believe,

G♭   **A♭**   **G♭** **A♭**
and I don't believe, and I don't

Repeat 4 times

‖: **D♭**   **G♭** **A♭**   :‖
care. (Whoo!) (Whoo!) (Whoo!) I don't

D♭   **A♭**   **G**

care.

IV. DEARLY BELOVED

Verse: **A♭**   **Cm**
Dearly Beloved are you listening?

D♭   **A♭**   **E♭**
I can't remember a word that you were saying.

A♭   **Cm**
Are we demented or am I disturbed?

D♭   **A♭**   **E♭**
The space that's in between insane and insecure.

A♭ **Cm**   **D♭**   **A♭** **E♭**
(Ooh.)   (Ooh.)

A♭   **Cm**
Oh, therapy, can you please fill the void?

D♭   **A♭**   **E♭**
Am I retarded or am I just overjoyed?

A♭   **Cm**
Nobody's perfect and I stand accused,

D♭   **A♭**   **E♭**
For lack of a better word and that's my best excuse.

A♭ **Cm**   **D♭**   **A♭** **E♭**
(Ooh.)   (Ooh.)

V. TALES OF ANOTHER BROKEN HOME

Riff A

A♭   G♭ D♭ A♭   G♭ D♭

A♭ *w/Riff A, 4 times*

Verse 1:   To live   and not to breathe

is   to   die in   tragedy.

To run,   to   run away

to find   what   you   believe.

       D♭ A♭ D♭ A♭ D♭   A♭ E♭   A♭ E♭ A♭ E♭
And   I   leave   behind

       D♭ A♭ D♭   A♭ D♭ A E♭ A♭ E♭ A♭ E♭
this   hurricane   of f***ing lies.

A♭ *w/Riff A, 4 times*

Verse 2:   I   lost   my   faith   to   this,

This   town   that   don't   exist.

So I   run,   I   run   away

to   the light   of   masochists.

       D♭ A♭ D♭ A♭ D♭   A♭ E♭   A♭ E♭ A♭ E♭
And   I   leave   behind

       D♭ A♭ D♭   A♭ D♭ A E♭ A♭ E♭ A♭ E♭
this   hurricane of f***ing lies.

       D♭ A♭ D♭ A♭ D♭   A♭   E♭ A♭ E♭ A♭ E♭
And   I   walked this   line

     D♭ A♭ D♭ A♭ D♭ A E♭ A♭ E♭ A♭ G♭ D♭ A♭
a   million and one f***ing times.   But not this time.

A♭   G♭ D♭ A♭   G♭ D♭

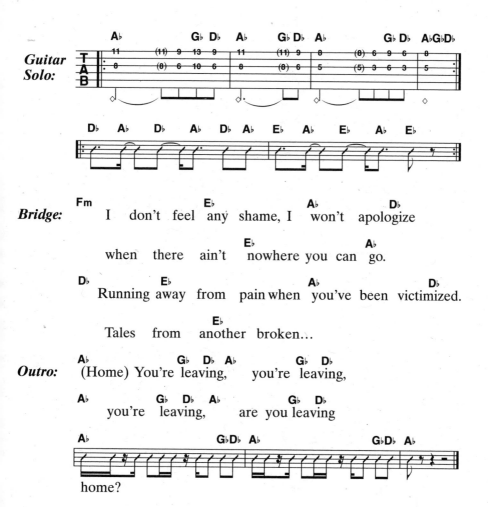

Guitar Solo:

Bridge:

Fm
I don't feel any shame, I

Eb
won't

Ab
apologize

Db

Eb
when there ain't nowhere you can

Ab
go.

Db
Running away from

Eb
pain when

Ab
you've been

Db
victimized.

Eb
Tales from another broken...

Outro:

Ab
(Home) You're leaving,

Gb   Db   Ab
you're leaving,

Gb   Db

Ab
you're leaving,

Gb   Db   Ab
are you leaving

Gb   Db

home?

KING FOR A DAY

Lyrics by BILLIE JOE
Music by BILLIE JOE and GREEN DAY

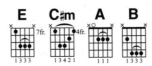

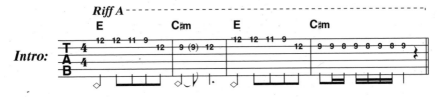

Intro:

Verse 1:

E
Started at the age of four.
C#m

E
My mother went to the groc'ry store.
C#m

E
Went sneaking through her bedroom door
C#m

E
to find something in a size four.
C#m

Pre-chorus:

A   B
Sugar and spice and ev'rything nice wasn't

A   B
meant for only girls.

A   B
G. I. Joe in pantyhose is

A   B
making room for the one and only

Chorus:

E   C#m
King for a day, princess by dawn.

E   C#m
King for a day, in a leather thong.

E   C#m
King for a day, princess by dawn.

A   B
Just wait 'til all the guys get a load of me.

w/Riff A

|E |C#m |E |C#m   ‖

Verse 2:
   E   C#m
My daddy threw me in therapy.

   E   C#m
He thinks I'm not a real man.

   E   C#m
Who put the drag in the drag queen?

   E   C#m
Don't knock it until you've tried it.

Pre-chorus:
  A   B
Sugar and spice and ev'rything nice wasn't

  A   B
meant for only girls.

  A   B
G. I. Joe in pantyhose is

  A   B
making room for the one and only

Chorus:
  E   C#m
King for a day, princess by dawn.

  E   C#m
King for a day in a leather thong.

  E   C#m
King for a day, princess by dawn.

  A   B
Just wait 'til all the guys get a load of me.

| E | C#m | E | C#m | ‖

    w/Riff A, simile   *Repeat 3 times*

Interlude: ‖: E | C#m | E | C#m :‖

Pre-chorus:
  A   B
Sugar and spice and ev'rything nice wasn't

  A   B
meant for only girls.

  A   B
G. I. Joe in pantyhose is

  A   B
making room for the one and only

	E				**C♯m**	

Chorus:

E   **C♯m**
King   for a day,   princess by dawn.

E   **C♯m**
King   for a day   in a leather thong.

E   **C♯m**
King   for a day,   princess by dawn.

E   **C♯m**
King   for a day   in a leather thong.

E   **C♯m**
King   for a day,   princess by dawn.

E   **C♯m**
King   for a day   in a leather thong.

E   **C♯m**
King   for a day,   princess by dawn.

A   **B**
Just   wait 'til all the guys,

A   **B**
Just   wait 'til all the guys,

A   **B**
Just wait 'til all the guys get a load of me.

w/Riff A, simile   *Repeat 4 times*

Outro: ‖: **E** |**C♯m** |**E** |**C♯m**   :‖ **E**   ‖

LAST OF THE AMERICAN GIRLS

Lyrics by BILLIE JOE
Music by GREEN DAY

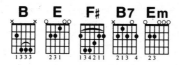

B

Verse 1: She puts her makeup   on like graffiti

                    E
on the walls   of the heartland.

               B
She's   got her little   book   of conspiracies

            F♯
right   in her hand.

        B
She is   paranoid, endangered   species

            E
headed   into extinction.

       B
She is   one of a   kind.

           F♯   **B**
Well, she's the last of the American girls.

          B
Verse 2: She wears   her overcoat for the

               E
coming of the nuclear   winter.

       B
She is   riding   her bike   like   a

               F♯
fugitive of critical   mass.

           B
She's   on a   hunger   strike   for the

                  E
ones   who won't make   it for dinner.

           B
She makes   enough to survive

                 F♯
for a   holiday of working class.

                  B   **B7**   **E**   **Em**

Chorus: She's a runaway of the establishment incorporated.

               B

She won't   cooperate.

               F♯   **B**

Well, she's   the last of the American girls.

   B   **E**   **B**   **E**   **B**   **E**   **B**   **E**

Riff A --

```
T
A  8   7   9  7    8  (8) 8   7   9  7   8   7   9  7   8  (8) 8   7   9  7
B
```

                B

Verse 3: She   plays   her vinyl   records,

                           E

singing songs   on the eve of destruction.

             B

She's   a sucker for all the criminals

              F♯

breaking the laws.

             B

She will   come in first for the

                   E

end of western civilization.

             B

She's   an endless war,

                          F♯

she's   a hero   for the lost cause.

             B   **B7**   **E**   **Em**

Chorus: Like a hurricane in the heart of the   devastation.

              B

She's   a nat'ral   disaster.

          F♯   **B**

She's   the last of the American girls.

  w/Riff A

  B   **E**   **B**   **E**   **B**   **E**   **B**   **E**

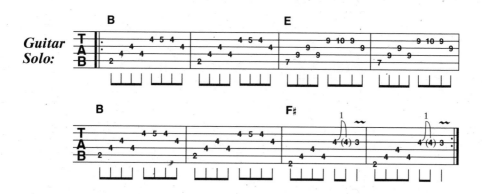

Guitar Solo:

Chorus:

                B   **B7**

She puts her makeup on like graffiti

                          E   **Em**

on the walls   of the heartland.

                  B   **B7**

She's   got her little book   of conspiracies

               F♯

right   in her hand.

              B

She will come in first for the

B7   **E**   **Em**

end of western civilization.

            B

She's a nat'ral disaster.

           F♯   **B**   **E**

She's the last of the American girls.

B **E**   **B** **E** **B** **E**   **B** **E**

    Oh yeah.   All right.

B **E**   **B** **E** **B** **E** **B**

    Oh yeah.

KNOW YOUR ENEMY

Lyrics by BILLIE JOE
Music by GREEN DAY

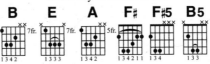

B   E   A   F♯   F♯5   B5

Intro:

| B | E | B | | B | E | B | A |

Chorus:

‖:
```
   B              E      B
   Do  you know  the  enemy?

              E    B
   Do you know  your enemy?
```
Repeat Chorus 3 times
```
   A    B       E    B      F♯
   Well, gotta  know the enemy. (Rah  eh!)
```
:‖

Verse 1:
```
   B           E      B             E      B
   Vi'lence is  an energy,  against  the enemy,

   A    B       E    B        F♯
   Well,  vi'lence is an energy. (Rah  eh!)

   B         E       B          E      B
   Bringing on the fury,    the choir   infantry,

   A B      E        B        F♯
   Revolt against the honor  to obey.  (Oh eh, oh eh.)
```

Verse 2:
```
   B          E      B          E      B
   Overthrow the effigy,    the vast  majority,

   A    B          E        B        F♯
   Well,  burning down  the foreman of control. (Oh eh, oh eh.)

   B        E    B           E      B
   Silence is the enemy,  against  your urgency,

   A B       E        B         F♯
   So rally up the demons of your soul.(Oh eh, oh eh.)
```

Chorus:

‖:
```
   B              E      B
   Do  you  know  the  enemy?

              E    B
   Do you know  your enemy?
```
Repeat Chorus 2 times
```
   A    B      E    B      F♯
   Well, gotta know the enemy. (Rah  eh!)
```
:‖

Bridge 1:
```
           E            B
   The  insurgency will  rise

            E                  B
   when   the blood's  been   sacrificed.
```

           E   B
We'll   be blinded by the lies

          F#5   B5 F#5   B5 F#5
in   your   eyes.   Say!

Guitar Solo:

(Oh, eh, oh, eh.)

Repeat 3 times

Riff A

Bridge 2: F#5 *w/Riff A, 4 times*
Well, vi'lence is an energy. (Oh eh, oh eh.)

Well,   from   here   to eternity. (Oh eh, oh eh.)

Well,   vi'lence is an energy, (Oh eh, oh eh.)

Well,   silence is the enemy, So, gimme, gimme revolution!

Interlude:
 B   E   B   B   E   B   A

Chorus: B   E   B
Do you know   the enemy?

             E   B
Do you know your enemy?

Repeat Chorus 3 times

A   B   E   B   F#
Well, gotta know the enemy. (Rah eh!)

Verse 3:
B   E   B   E   B
Overthrow the effigy, the vast majority,

A   B   E   B   F#
Well, burning down the foreman of control. (Oh eh, oh eh.)

B   E   B   E   B
Silence is the enemy, against your urgency,

A B   E   B   F#   B
So rally up the demons of your soul.(Oh eh, oh eh.)

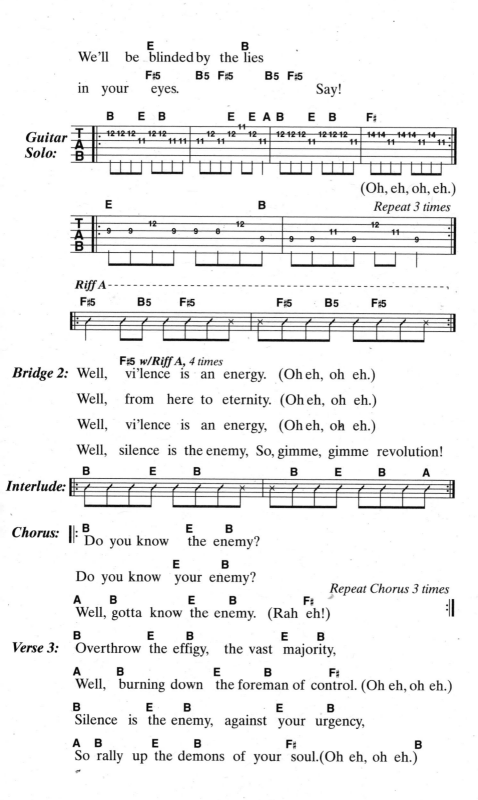

LAST NIGHT ON EARTH

Lyrics by BILLIE JOE
Music by GREEN DAY

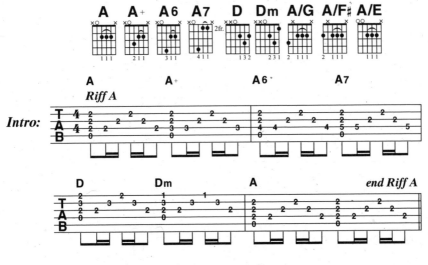

Verse 1:

A		A+		A6		A7

I text a postcard sent to you. Did it go through?

D   **Dm**   **A**
Sending all my love to you.

A   **A+**   **A6**   **A7**
You are the moonlight of my life ev'ry night.

D   **Dm**   **A**
Giving all my love to you.

Chorus:

D   **Dm**   **A**
My beating heart belongs to you.

D   **Dm**   **A**
I walked for miles 'til I found you.

D   **Dm**
I'm here to honor you.

A   **A/G**   **A/F♯**   **A/E**   **D**
If I lose ev'rything in the fire,

w/Riff A

     Dm   **A**   **A+** **A6** **A7** **D** **Dm** **A**
I'm sending all my love to you.

Verse 2:

A   **A+**   **A6**   **A7**
With ev'ry breath that I am worth here on earth,

D   **Dm**   **A**
I'm sending all my love to you.

A   A+   D6   D7
So if you dare to second guess, you could rest

D   Dm   A
assured that all my love's for you.

Chorus: D   Dm   A
My beating heart belongs to you.

D   Dm   A
I walked for miles 'til I found you.

D   Dm
I'm here to honor you.

A   A/G   A/F♯   A/E   D
If I lose   ev'rything in the fire,

            Dm
I'm sending all my love to you.

w/Riff A

Guitar
Solo: ‖: A   A+ |A6   A7 |D   Dm |A   :‖

Chorus: D   Dm   A
My beating heart belongs to you.

D   Dm   A
I walked for miles 'til I found you.

D   Dm
I'm here to honor you.

A   A/G   A/F♯   A/E   D
If I lose   ev'rything in the fire,

        Dm
did I ever   make it through?

Outro:

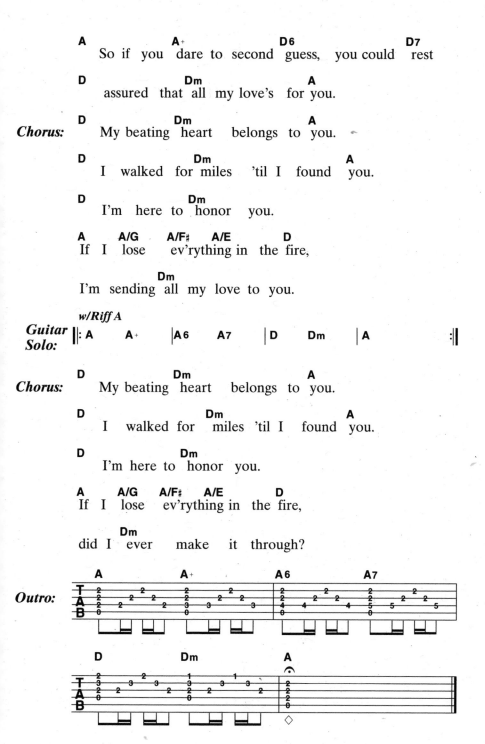

LONGVIEW

Lyrics by BILLIE JOE
Music by GREEN DAY

To match recording,
tune down 1/2 step:
⑥ = Eb ③ = Gb
⑤ = Ab ② = Bb
④ = Db ① = Eb

E   D   B   A

Intro:

Riff A

Verse 1:

E   D   E   D
I sit around and watch the tube, but nothing's on.

E   D   E   D
I change the channels for an hour or two,

E   D   E
Twiddle my thumbs just for a bit.

            D   E
I'm sick of all the same old s***;

        D   E   D
In a house with unlocked doors, and I'm f***ing lazy.

Chorus:

B   A   E   B
Bite my lip and close my eyes.

        A   E
Take me away to paradise.

B   A   E   B
I'm so damn bored I'm going blind

                      w/Riff A
                 A | E | D | E | D
And I smell like s***.

Verse 2:

E   D   E   D
Peel me off this Velcro seat and get me moving.

E   D   E   D
I sure as hell can't do it by myself.

E   D   E
I'm feeling like a dog in heat

        D   E
Barred indoors from the summer street.

        D   E   D
I locked the door to my own cell and I lost the key.

Chorus:
```
B              A        E          B
Bite  my  lip  and close    my  eyes.

              A            E
Take    me  away    to  paradise.

B                  A        E          B
  I'm so  damn    bored  I'm going    blind

                      A
And      I    smell    like s***.
```

Bridge:
```
E           D          E           D
I    got no  motivation.  Where is   my motivation?

E            D            E           D
No time    for a  motivation.  Smoking  my  inspiration.
```

Interlude:
```
              Repeat 3 times                  w/Riff A
‖: B      | A  E  :‖ B     | A     | E    | D    | E    | D    ‖
```

Verse 3:
```
E           D                    E                D
I   sit around  and watch  the phone  but no one's   calling.

E            D            E           D
Call me pathetic, call me  what you  will.

E                D            E
My    mother  says to  get a   job,

               D                    E
But  she  don't  like  the   one she's got.

               D            E                 D  | D   A‖
When masturbation's lost its fun, you're f***ing lonely.|
```

Chorus:
```
B              A        E          B
  Bite   my lip  and  close    my  eyes.

              A        E
Take    me  away    to  paradise.

B                  A          E          B
  I'm so  damn    bored,  I'm going    blind

                A        E
And      loneliness has to  suffice.

B              A        E          B
  Bite   my lip  and close    my  eyes,

               A        E
Oh,     slippin'  away    to  paradise.

B              A        E        B
  Some   say  quit  or  I'll  go  blind,
                    w/Riff A                    Repeat and fade
                 A  ‖: E       | D        | E       | D        :‖
But it's  just a  myth.|
```

MACY'S DAY PARADE

Words by BILLIE JOE
Music by GREEN DAY

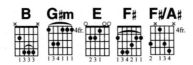

Intro:

    B

Verse 1:

B
Today's the Macy's Day Parade.

G#m
The night of the living dead is on its way,

E   F#   B
with a credit report for duty call.

It's a lifetime guarantee,

G#m
stuffed in a coffin, "ten percent more free."

E   F#   B
Red - light special at the mausoleum.

Pre-chorus:

E
Give me something that I need,

F#   E
satisfaction guaranteed to you.

What's the consolation prize?

F#   B
Economy - sized dreams of hope.

Verse 2:

B
When I was a kid I thought

G#m
I wanted all the things that I haven't got.

E   F#   B
Oh, but I learned the hardest way.

G#m
Then I realized what it took

                                                   E
to tell the diff'rence between thieves and crooks.

        F♯   **B**
Let's learn, me and you.

      E
Pre-chorus: Give me something that I need,

        F♯

        satisfaction guaranteed.

               B   **F♯/A♯**   **G♯m**
Chorus: 'Cause I'm thinking 'bout a brand - new hope,

        F♯   **E**
the one I've never known.

             F♯   **B**
'Cause now I know it's all that I wanted.

Instrumental:
  ‖: B | | **G♯m** | | **E** | **F♯** | **B** | :‖

      E
Pre-chorus: What's the consolation prize?

     F♯   **B**
        Economy-sized   dreams of hope.

      E

        Give me something that I need,

      F♯

        satisfaction guaranteed.

               B   **F♯/A♯**   **G♯m**
Chorus: 'Cause I'm thinking 'bout a brand - new hope,

        F♯   **E**   **F♯**
the one I've never known and where it goes.

        B   **F♯/A♯ G♯m**
And I'm thinking 'bout the only road,

        F♯   **E**   **F♯**
the one I've never known and where it goes.

        B   **F♯/A♯**   **G♯**
And I'm thinking 'bout a brand new hope,

        F♯   **E**
the one I've never known

             F♯   **B**
'cause now I know it's all that I wanted.

MARIA

Lyrics by BILLIE JOE
Music by GREEN DAY

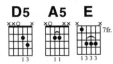

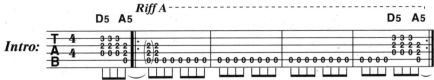

Verse 1:
A5 *w/Riff A, 2 times, simile*   **D5**
She smashed the radio with the board of education.

A5
Turn up the static left of the state of the nation.

Pre-chorus:
E
Turn up the flame, step on the gas.

Burning the flag at half mast.

She's a rebel's forgotten son.

                                        D5
An export of the revolution.

Verse 2:
A5 *w/Riff A, 2 times, simile*   **D5**
She is the first voice of the last ones in the line.

A5
She'll drag the lake to keep the vendetta alive.

Pre-chorus:
E
Bring in the head of the government.

The dog ate the document.

Somebody shot the president,

And no one knows where Maria went.

Chorus:
D5 A5   **D5 A5**   **D5 A5**
Ma-ri - a,   Ma-ri - a,   Ma-ri - a,

                    E
where did you go?

Interlude:

| E   A5 | E   A5 | E   A5 | E   A5 ||

        E   A5   E A5
Bridge: Be careful what you're offering,

          E   A5   E   A5
your   breath lacks a   conviction.

E   A5   E   A5
Drawing the line in the dirt,

     E   A5   E
because the last decision was...

Guitar Solo:

no!

A5 *w/Riff A, 2 times, simile*   D5
Verse 3:   She smashed the radio with the board of education.

A5
Turn up the static left of the state of the nation.

   E
Pre-chorus: Turn up the flame, step on the gas.

Burning the flag at half mast.

She's a rebel's forgotten son.

An export of the revolution.

       D5 A5   D5 A5   D5 A5
Chorus: Ma-ri - a,   Ma-ri - a,   Ma-ri - a,

                E
where did you go?

    D5 A5   D5 A5   D5 A5
Ma-ri - a,   Ma-ri - a,   Ma-ri - a,

                E
where did you go?

Outro:

MURDER CITY

Lyrics by BILLE JOE
Music by GREEN DAY

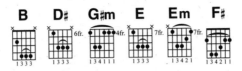

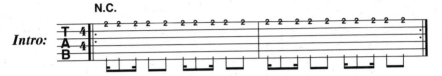

Intro:

Chorus:
B   D♯
Desperate, but not hopeless.

G♯m   E   Em
    I feel so useless in the murder city.

B   D♯
Desperate, but not helpless.

G♯m   E   Em
    The clock strikes midnight in the murder city.

Verse 1:
B   D♯   G♯m
    I'm wide   awake   after   the riots.

E   B   F♯
This demonstration of our anguish.

B   D♯   G♯m
This empty laughter has no reason,

E   B   F♯
Like a bottle   of your fav'rite poison.

E   Em
    We are the last call and we're so pathetic.

Chorus:
B   D♯
Desperate, but not hopeless.

G♯m   E   Em
    I feel so useless in the murder city.

B   D♯
Desperate, but not helpless.

G♯m   E   Em
    The clock strikes midnight in the murder city.

Guitar Solo: ‖: B | D♯ | G♯m | E | Em :‖

Verse 2:

B   D♯   G♯m
Christians crying in the bathroom

E   B   F♯
And I just want to bum a cigarette.

B   D♯   G♯m
We've come so far, we've been so wasted.

E   B   F♯
It's written all over our faces.

                               Drums --
E   Em | N.C.
We are the last call and we're so pathetic.   ‖

Chorus:

B   D♯
Desperate, but not hopeless.

G♯m   E   Em
I feel so useless in the murder city.

B   D♯
Desperate, but not helpless.

G♯m   E   Em
The clock strikes midnight in the murder city.

B   D♯
Desperate, but not hopeless.

G♯m   E   Em
I feel so useless in the murder city.

B   D♯
Desperate, but not helpless.

G♯m   E
The clock strikes midnight in the...

MINORITY

Lyrics by BILLIE JOE
Music by GREEN DAY

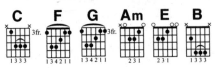

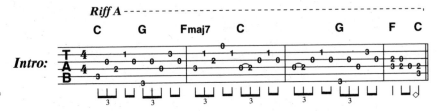

Chorus:
    C   **F**   **G** **F**
I want to be the mi - nori - ty.

    C   **F**   **G**   **F**
I don't need your au - thori - ty.

    C   **F**   **G** **F**
Down with the moral ma - jori - ty.

        C   **F**   **G** **F**
'Cause I want to be the mi - nori - ty.

Verse 1:
  C   **G**   **F**   **C**
I pledge allegiance to the underworld.

            G   **F**   **G**
One nation underdog there of which I stand alone.

    C   **G**   **F**   **C**
A face in the crowd, unsung against the mold.

         F   **G**   **C**
Without a doubt, singled out, the only way I know.

Chorus:
      C   **F**   **G** **F**
'Cause I want to be the mi - nori - ty.

    C   **F**   **G** **F**
I don't need your au - thori - ty.

    C   **F**   **G** **F**
Down with the moral ma - jori - ty.

      C   **F**   **G** **F**
'Cause I want to be the mi - nori - ty.

Bridge:
Am   E F C
Stepped out of the line

Am   E   F   G
like a sheep runs from the herd.

Am   E F C
Marching out of time

Am   F   G   B
to my own beat now. The only way I know.

Verse 2:
           C   G   F   C
One light, one mind flashing in the dark.

               G   F   G
Blinded by the silence of a thousand broken hearts.

          C   G   F   C
"For crying out loud," she screamed unto me.

              F   G   C
A free-for-all, f*** 'em all. "You are your own sight."

Chorus:
           C   F   G F
'Cause I want to be the mi-nori-ty.

C   F   G F
I don't need your au-thori-ty.

C   F   G F
Down with the moral ma-jori-ty.

           C   F   G F
'Cause I want to be the mi-nori-ty.

Instrumental Bridge:

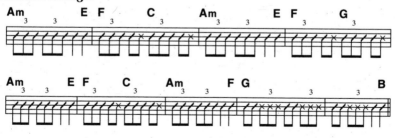

Interlude: | C   G | F   C | G | F   G ||

Verse 3:

```
       C          G      F            C
One   light,  one  mind  flashing in the dark.

              G          F            G
Blinded by the silence of a thousand  broken hearts.

         C       G      F            C
"For   crying  out loud," she screamed unto me.

            F            G                C
A  free-for-all, f***'em all.  "You are your own sight."
```

Chorus:

```
          C              F       G   F
'Cause  I  want   to  be the mi-nori-ty.

C        F              G   F
I  don't  need  your   au-thori-ty.

C        F              G   F
Down  with the moral  ma-jori-ty.

         C        F       G   F
'Cause  I  want to  be the mi-nori-ty.

C           F       G   F
I  want  to  be the mi-nori-ty.

C           F       G   F
I  want  to  be the mi-nori-ty.

C           F       G   F
I  want  to  be the mi-nori-ty.

C           F       G   F
I  want  to  be the mi-nori-ty.
```

w/Riff A

Outro: | C   G | Fmaj7 C | G | F   C   ‖

NICE GUYS FINISH LAST

Lyrics by BILLIE JOE
Music by BILLIE JOE and GREEN DAY

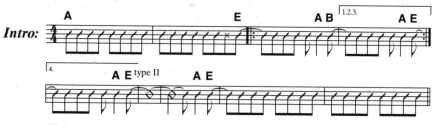

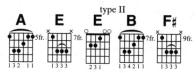

Verse 1:
   E
Nice guys finish last. You're running out of gas.

     B   **E**   **A**
Your sympathy will get you left behind.

Sometimes you're at your best when you feel the worst.

     B   **E**
You feel washed-up, like piss going down the drain.

Pre-chorus:
A   **E**
Pressure cooker, pick my brain and tell me I'm insane.

A   **E**
I'm so f***ing happy, I could cry.

A
Ev'ry joke can have its truth,

   E
but now the joke's on you.

   F#   **B**
I never knew you're such a funny guy.

Chorus:
    E   **A**
Oh, nice guys finish last,

    E   **A**
when you are the outcast.

    E   **A**
Don't pat yourself on the back,

           B   **A**
you might break your spine.

Verse 2:
E
Living on command. You're shaking lots of hands.

    B   E   A
You're kissing up and bleeding all your   trust.

E
Taking what you need. Bite the hand that feeds.

    B   E
You'll lose your memory and you got no shame.

Pre-chorus:
A   E
Pressure cooker, pick my brain and tell me I'm insane.

A   E
I'm so f***ing happy, I could cry.

A
Ev'ry joke can have its truth,

     E
but now the joke's on you.

   F#   B
I never knew you're such a funny guy.

Chorus:
     E   A
Oh, nice guys finish last,

     E   A
when you are the outcast.

        E   A
Don't pat yourself on the back,

              B
you might break your spine.

                A
Oh, nice guys finish last,

     E   A
when you are the outcast.
        E   A
Don't pat yourself on the back,

              B   A
you might break your spine.

Instrumental:

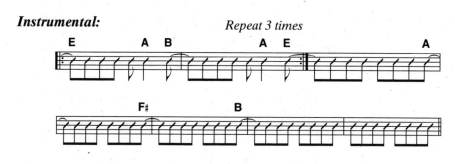

Repeat 3 times

Chorus:

       E   **A**
Oh,   nice   guys finish last,

      E   **A**
when   you are the outcast.

         E   **A**
Don't pat yourself on the back,

                    B
you might break your   spine.

                    A
Oh,   nice   guys finish last,

      E   **A**
when   you are the outcast.

         E   **A**
Don't pat yourself on the back,

Outro:

                 B   **A**   **E**   **A** **E**
you might break your spine.

ONE FOR THE RAZORBACKS

Lyrics by BILLIE JOE
Music by GREEN DAY

To match recording,
tune down 1/2 step:
⑥ = E♭ ③ = G♭
⑤ = A♭ ② = B♭
④ = D♭ ① = E♭

C   G   F

Intro:

Verse 1:
> C   G   C   F
> Juliet's trying to find out what she wants,
>
> C   G   C   G
> but she don't know. Experience has got her down.
>
> C   G   C   F
> Well, look this direction; I know it's not perfection,
>
> C   G   C
> it's just me. I want to bring you up again, now.

Chorus:
> G   F   C
> 'Cause I'm losing what's left of my dignity.
>
> G   F   C
> A small price I'll pay to see that you're happy.
>
> G   F   C
> Forget all the disappointments you have faced.
>
> G   F   C
> Open up your worried world and let me in.

Verse 2:
> C   G   C   F
> Juliet's crying 'cause now she's realizing
>
> C   G   C   G
> Love can be filled with pain and distrust.
>
> C   G   C   F
> I know I am crazy and a bit lazy
>
> C   G   C
> But I will try to bring you up again somehow.

Chorus:
         G   F   C
'Cause I'm losing what's left of my dignity.

             G   F   C
A small price I'll pay to see that you're happy.

         G   F   C
Forget all the disappointments you have faced.

        G   F   C
Open up your worried world and let me in.

Guitar Solo: ‖: C | G | C | F | C | G | C | G :‖ C | ‖
(1. .... 2. ....)

Verse 3:
     C   G   C   F
Juliet's crying 'cause now she's realizing

           C   G   C   G
Love can be filled with pain and distrust.

     C   G   C   F
I know I am crazy and a bit lazy

           C   G   C
But I will try to bring you up again somehow.

Chorus:
         G   F   C
'Cause I'm losing what's left of my dignity.

             G   F   C
A small price I'll pay to see that you're happy.

        G   F   C
Forget all the disappointments you have faced.

        G   F   C
Open up your worried world and let me in.

THE ONE I WANT

Lyrics by BILLIE JOE
Music by GREEN DAY

To match recording,
tune down 1/2 step:
⑥ = E♭   ③ = G♭
⑤ = A♭   ② = B♭
④ = D♭   ① = E♭

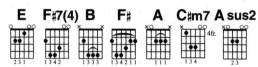

E   F#7(4)   B   F#   A   C#m7   A sus2

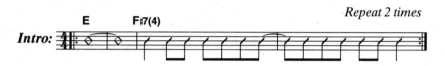

Repeat 2 times

Intro:
E   F#7(4)

Verse 1:

B   F#
Sitting   in   my room   last night,

A   E
Staring   at   the   mirror.

B   F#
I   couldn't   find   a reason   why

A   E
I   couldn't   be   near   her.

Pre-chorus:

C#m7   A sus2
'Cause   you are   the   one that started

B
To   make   me feel this way.

C#m7   A sus2
And   ev'ry   night,   I'm   thinking

B
About   those words   you'd   say.

Verse 2:

B   F#
Of pictures going   through my mind

A   E
When   we're   together.

B   F#
All these   long and   sleepless nights.

A   E
Will   I   ever   get   better?

Pre-chorus:

C#m7   A sus2
'Cause you are the one that started

B
To make me feel this way.

C#m7   A sus2
And ev'ry night, I'm thinking

B
About those words you'd say.

Chorus: ||: *Repeat 4 times*

        E   F#7(4)
'Cause you are the one that I want. :||

Verse 3:

B   F#
Now you know how I feel.

A   E
This love is forever.

B   F#
You make my life seem so unreal.

A   E
Will I ever get better?

Pre-chorus:

C#m7   A sus2
'Cause you are the one that started

B
To make me feel this way.

C#m7   A sus2
And ev'ry night, I'm thinking

B
About those words you'd say.

Chorus: ||: *Repeat 4 times*

        E   F#7(4)
'Cause you are the one that I want. :||

Guitar Solo:

B	F#	A	E	B	F#	A	E
C#m7	A sus2	B		C#m7	A sus2	B	
C#m7	A sus2	B		C#m7	A sus2	B		

Chorus: ||: *Repeat 4 times*

        E   F#7(4)
'Cause you are the one that I want. :|| B ||

ONE OF MY LIES

Lyrics by BILLIE JOE
Music by GREEN DAY

To match recording,
tune down 1/2 step:
⑥ = E♭   ③ = G♭
⑤ = A♭   ② = B♭
④ = D♭   ① = E♭

D5 A5 G5 F#5 B5

Intro:

| D5 | A5 | | G5 F#5 | G5 F#5 G5 A5 |

Verse 1:

D5
When   I   was   A5 younger,

B5   F#5
I   thought that the   world circled   around   me.

G5   D5   A5
But in   time,   I   realized I   was so   wrong.

D5   A5   B5
My immortal thoughts turned   into just dreams

F#5
of   a   dead   future.

G5   D5   A5
It   was a   tragic case of   my reality,   yeah.

Pre-chorus:

G5   A5
Do you   think   you're   indestructible

G5   A5
and   no   one   can touch   you?

G5   A5
Well,   I   think   you're   disposable

G5   A5
and   it's   time   you   knew   the truth.

Chorus:

D5   B5 A5
'Cause   it's just one of   my   lies.

D5   B5 A5
But   it's just one   of   my lies.

D5   B5 A5
And   all   I   want   to   do   is   get real   high.

D5   B5 A5
But   it's just one   of   my lies.

Verse 2:

D5   A5   B5
Why does   my life have   to   be   so   small?

F#5
And   death   is   forever?

          G5   **D5**   **A5**
And   does forever have a life to call its own?

D5   **A5**   **B5**
Don't give me an answer, 'cause you only know

                  F♯5
as much   as I   know.

          G5
Unless you've been   there   once,

     D5   **A5**
Well,   I hardly think   so.

            G5   **A5**
Pre-chorus: Do you think you're   indestructible

     G5   **A5**
and no one can touch   you?

        G5   **A5**
Well,   I think   you're disposable

        G5   **A5**
and it's time you knew the truth.

                        D5   **B5 A5**
Chorus: 'Cause it's just one of my lies.

                    D5   **B5 A5**
But it's just one of my lies.

                        D5   **B5 A5**
And all I want   to do is get real high.

                  D5   **B5 A5**
But it's just one of my lies.

        F♯5 G5 A5
Bridge: I   used   to pray   at

F♯5 G5 A5
night,   before   I   lay myself

F♯5   G5 A5
down.   My mother said he was

F♯5   G5 A5
right,   her mother said it too?

Repeat 2 times

      D5   **B5 A5**   **D5**   **B5 A5**

Interlude:

(1st time) Why?

Repeat 4 times

      D5   **A5**   **G5 F♯5**   **G5**   **F♯5 G5 A5**   **D5**

Outro:

ONLY OF YOU

To match recording,
tune down 1/2 step:
⑥ = E♭ ③ = G♭
⑤ = A♭ ② = B♭
④ = D♭ ① = E♭

Lyrics by BILLIE JOE
Music by GREEN DAY

F♯5   A5   D5   B5   A   B   Dsus2   E5   E5 (type II)   D

Intro:

Riff A - ,
Repeat 4 times

F♯5   A5   D5   A5   B5

Riff B - ,
Repeat 2 times

A   B   Dsus2   E5

w/Riff B, *4 times*

Verse 1:
    A   **B**
    I wish I could tell you,

Dsus2   **E5**
But the words would come out wrong.

    A   **B**
    God, if you only knew

Dsus2   **E5**
The way I've felt for so long.

    A   **B**
    I know that we're worlds apart,

Dsus2   **E5**
But I just don't seem to care.

    A   **B**
    These feelings in my heart,

Dsus2   **E5**
Only with you I want to share.

w/Riff A, *4 times*

Chorus:
  F♯5   **F♯5**
The first time I caught a glimpse of you,

F♯5   **F♯5**
Then all my thoughts were only of you.

Interlude:
w/Riff B   *Repeat 2 times*

‖: A   B | | D sus2   E5 | :‖

(1st time) Ah.

Verse 2:

w/Riff B, 4 times

A   B
I hope that when time goes by

D sus2   E5
You will think the same about me.

A   B
Many nights awake I lie,

D sus2   E5
I only wish that you could see.

A   B
I know that we're only friends.

D sus2   E5
I hope this feeling never ends.

A   B
If I could only hold you,

D sus2   E5
It's the only thing I want to do.

Chorus:

w/Riff A, 4 times

F♯5   F♯5
The first time I caught a glimpse of you,

F♯5   F♯5
Then all my thoughts were only of you.

Bridge:

Ah.

Repeat 4 times

Guitar Solo:

Outro:

Whoa! (3rd & 4th time)

PAPER LANTERNS

Lyrics by BILLIE JOE
Music by GREEN DAY

To match recording,
tune down one whole step:
⑥ = D   ③ = F
⑤ = G   ② = A
④ = C   ① = D

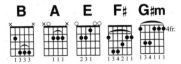

B   A   E   F♯   G♯m

1 3 3 3   1 1 1   2 3 1   1 3 4 2 1 1   1 3 4 1 1 1

Repeat 4 times

Riff A -

B   **A**   **E**   **B**

Intro: 𝄆 / / × / / × / / / / × 𝄇

Verse 1:
B				F♯			
Now	I	rest	my	head	from	such	an

E   **B**
Endless dreary   time.

                                          A
A time   of hopes and happiness that

E   **B**
Had you on my mind.

                                          F♯
Those days are gone and now it seems   as

E   **B**
If   I'll get some   rest.

                                          A
But now and   then I'll see you again, and it

E   **B**
Puts my heart to the test.

Chorus:
	E			F♯			B
So	when	are all my	troubles	going	to	end?	

        E   **F♯**   **B**   **G♯m**
I'm understanding now that we are only friends.

              A   **E**
To this day, I'm asking why I   still   think about

w/Riff A, 2 times

Interlude: | B   A   E | B | B   A   E | B ‖
you.

         B   **F♯**
Verse 2: As the days   go on, I   wonder

         E   **B**
         Will this ever end?

                       A
         I find it hard to keep   control when

         E   **B**
         You're with your boyfriend.

                     F♯
         I do not mind if all I   am is

         E   **B**
         Just a friend to you.

                     A
         But all I want to know right now is if you

         E   **B**
         Think about me too.

            E   **F♯**   **B**
Chorus: So when are all my troubles going to end?

              E   **F♯**   **B**   **G♯m**
         I'm understanding now that we are only friends.

             A   **E**
         To this day, I'm asking why I still think about

         w/Riff A, 4 times
Interlude: |B A E| B |B A E| B |B A E| B |B A E| B ‖
         you.   you.

         w/Riff A, 4 times
Guitar
Solo: |B A E| B |B A E| B |B A E| B |B A E| B ‖

            E   **F♯**   **B**
Chorus: So when are all my troubles going to end?

             E   **F♯**   **B**   **G♯m**
         I'm understanding now that we are only friends.

             A   **E**
         To this day, I'm asking why I still think about

         w/Riff A, 4 times
Outro: |B A E| B |B A E| B |B A E| B |B A E| B ‖
         you.

PEACEMAKER

Lyrics by BILLE JOE
Music by GREEN DAY

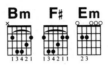

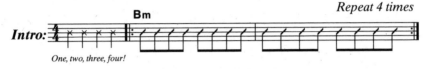

Repeat 4 times

Intro:

One, two, three, four!

Bm
Verse 1: Well, I've got a fever, a nonbeliever.

I'm in a state of grace.

                                        F#
For I am the Caesar. I'm gonna seize the day.

Well, call of the banshee, hey hey, hey hey hey hey hey.

                                      Bm
As God as my witness, the infidels are gonna pay.

Bm
Verse 2: Well, call the assassin, the orgasm,

a spasm of love and hate.

                                        F#
For what will divide us? The righteous and the meek.

Well, call of the wild, hey hey, hey hey hey hey hey.

                                      Bm
Well, death to the girl at the end of the serenade.

       F#   **Bm**
Chorus: Vendetta, sweet vendetta, this Beretta of the night.

           Em   **Bm**
This fire and the desire.

           F#   **Bm**
Well, shots ringing out on the holy parasite.

Verse 3:   **Bm**
Well, I am a killjoy from Detroit,

I drink from a well of rage.

                                 F♯
I feed off the weakness with all my love.

Well, call up the captain, hey, hey, hey, hey, hey, hey, hey.

                                                 Bm
Well, death to the lover that you were dreaming of.

Verse 4:   **Bm**
Well, this is a standoff,

a Molotov cocktail's on the house.

                                   F♯
You thought I was a write - off, you better think again.

Well, call the peacemaker. Hey, hey, hey, hey, hey, hey, hey.

                                        Bm
I'm gonna send you back to the place where it all began.

Chorus: **F♯**   **Bm**
Vendetta, sweet vendetta, this Beretta of the night.

         Em   **Bm**
This fire and the desire.

        F♯   **Bm**
Well, shots ringing out on the holy parasite.

Freely - - - - - - ‚ *Guitar Solo:*

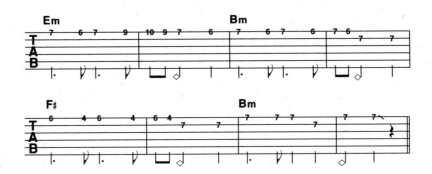

Verse 5:

Bm
Well,　now the caretakers,　the undertakers

Saw　I'm gonna　go out and get a　peacemaker.

　　　　　　　　　　　　　　　　　　F♯
This　　is a　neo-Saint　Valentines　massacre.

Well,　　call up the Gaza,　hey, hey,　　hey, hey, hey, hey, hey.

　　　　　　　　　　　　　　　　　　　　　　Bm
. Well,　　death　to the ones at the end of the serenade.

　　　　F♯　　　　　　　　　　　　　　**Bm**
Well,　death　to the ones at the end of the serenade.

　　　　F♯　　　　　　　　　　　　　　**Bm**
Well,　death　to the ones at the end of the serenade.

　　　Freely -,
　　　　F♯
. 　Well,　death　to the ones at the end of the serenade.

atempo
Bm

Outro:

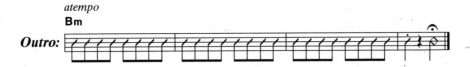

RESTLESS HEART SYNDROME

Lyrics by BILLIE JOE
Music by GREEN DAY

To match recording,
tune down one whole step:
⑥ = D   ③ = F
⑤ = G   ② = A
④ = C   ① = D

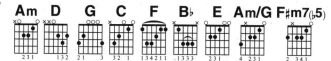

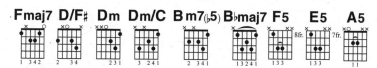

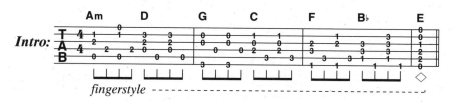

fingerstyle -

Verse 1:

Am   Am/G   F♯m7(♭5) Fmaj7
I've got a   really   bad disease.

Am   Am/G   D/F♯   F
It's got me begging on my hands and knees.

Am Am/G F♯m7(♭5) Fmaj7
So take me to   emergency,

Am   Am/G   D/F♯ F
'cause something seems to be missing.

Am   Am/G   F♯m7(♭5) Fmaj7
Somebody take the pain away.

Am   Am/G   D/F♯   Fmaj7
It's like an ulcer   bleeding in my brain.

Am   Am/G F♯m7(♭5) Fmaj7
So send me to the pharmacy,

Am   Am/G   D/F♯ Fmaj7
so I can lose my memory.

Pre-chorus:

Dm Dm/C B m7(♭5) B♭maj7
I'm elated, medicated.

Dm   Dm/C   B m7(♭5) B♭maj7   E
Lord knows, I tried to find a way   to run away.

Verse 2:

| Am | | Am/G | | F#m7(b5) | Fmaj7 |

. I think they found another cure

Am   Am/G   D/F#   F

For broken hearts and feeling insecure.

Am   Am/G F#m7(b5) Fmaj7

You'd be surprised what I endure.

Am   Am/G   D/F# F

What makes you feel so self-assured?

Am   Am/G   F#m7(b5) Fmaj7

I need to find a place to hide.

Am   Am/G   D/F#   Fmaj7

You never know what could be waiting outside.

Am Am/G   F#m7(b5)   Fmaj7

The accidents that you could find.

Am   Am/G   D/F# Fmaj7

It's like some kind of suicide.

Pre-chorus:

Dm   Dm/C Bm7(b5)   Bbmaj7

So what ails you what impales you.

Dm   Dm/C   Bm7(b5) Bbmaj7   E

I feel like I've been crucified to be satisfied.

Chorus:

Am   Am/G

I'm a victim of my symptom.

F#m7(b5)   D   G E

I am my own worst enemy.

Am   Am/G

You're a victim of your symptom.

F#m7(b5)   D   G

You are your own worst enemy.

E

Know your enemy.

Repeat 4 times

Guitar Solo:

| Am | Am/G | F#m7(b5) | F5 | E5 |

Chorus:

     Am   Am/G
I'm elated,   medicated.

F#m7(b5)   D   G   E
I am my own worst   enemy.

Am   Am/G
So what ails you   s'what impales you.

F#m7(b5)   D   G   E
You are your own worst enemy.

Am   Am/G
You're a victim   of the system.

F#m7(b5)   D   G   E
You are your own worst enemy.

Am   Am/G
You're a victim   of the system.

F#m7(b5)   D   G   E
You are your own worst enemy.

Repeat 4 times

Outro:

PRIVATE ALE

Lyrics by BILLIE JOE
Music by GREEN DAY

To match recording,
tune down 1/2 step:
⑥ = E♭ ③ = G♭
⑤ = A♭ ② = B♭
④ = D♭ ① = E♭

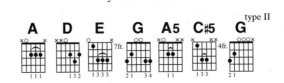

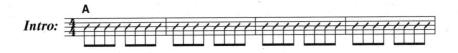

Intro:

Verse 1:

     A
I wander down these streets all by myself.

          D
Think of my future, now I just don't know.

      A
Well, I don't seem to care.

I stop to notice that I'm by your home.

        D
I wonder if you're sitting all alone,

      A
Or is your boyfriend there?

Chorus:

     D **A** **E**
Because I feel so right,

   D **A** **E**
let my imagination go.

    D **A** **E**
Until you're in my sight,

     D   **A**   **E**
and through my veins temptation flows. Wha -

|**A** |**G D** |**A** |**G D** |**A** |**G D** |**A** |**G D** ‖
oh.   Oh, yeah.

Verse 2:
        A
So I sit down here on the hard concrete.

                           D
Think of my future, now I just don't know,

                 A
Well, I don't seem to care.

I stop to notice that I'm by your home.

                    D
I wonder if you're sitting all alone,

              A
Or is your boyfriend there?

          D   **A** **E**
Chorus: Because I feel so right,

          D   **A**   **E**
let my imagination go.

          D **A** **E**
Until you're in my sight,

          D   **A**   **E**
and through my veins temptation flows. Wha -

| A | G D | A | G D | A | G D | A | G D ‖

oh.   Oh, yeah.

Interlude:

Repeat 2 times — A5 C#5 G type II   A5 C#5 G type II

Repeat 4 times — E   A   D

           Wha!
          D   **A** **E**
Chorus: Because I feel so right,

          D   **A**   **E**
let my imagination go.

          D **A** **E**
Until you're in my sight,

          D   **A**   **E**
and through my veins temptation flows. Wha -

                                     type II
| A | G D | A | G D | A | G D | A | G D | A5 C#5 G ‖

oh.   Oh, yeah.

SEE THE LIGHT

Lyrics by BILLIE JOE
Music by GREEN DAY

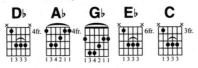

Repeat 4 times

Intro: Db   Ab

Verse 1:
             Db   Ab   Db   Ab
Well, I crossed the river, fell into the sea,

             Db Ab   Db   Ab
where the nonbelievers go beyond belief.

            Db   Ab   Db   Ab
Then I scratched the surface in the mouth of hell,

           Db   Ab   Db   Ab
running out of service, in the blood I fell.

Chorus:
            Db   Gb   Db   Ab   Db Ab
Well, I, I just want to see the light.

         Db   Gb   Db   Ab   Db Ab
And I, I don't want to lose my sight.

         Db   Gb   Db   Ab   Db Ab
Well, I, I just want to see the light.

      Db   Gb   Db   Eb | Ab Eb Ab C ‖
And I need to know what's worth the fight.

Verse 2:
Db   Ab   Db Ab
I've been wasted, pills and alcohol,

      Db   Ab   Db   Ab
and I've been chasing down the pool halls.

         Db   Ab   Db Ab
Then I drank the water from a hurricane,

        Db   Ab   Db   Ab
and I set a fire just to see the flame.

Chorus:
            Db   Gb   Db   Ab   Db Ab
Well, I, I just want to see the light.

         Db   Gb   Db   Ab   Db Ab
And I, I don't want to lose my sight.

          D♭   **G♭**   **D♭**   **A♭**   **D♭** **A♭**
Well, I, I just want   to see the light.

          D♭   **G♭**   **D♭**   **E♭**
And I need   to know   what's   worth   the fight.

Repeat 3 times

Guitar Solo:

Verse 3: Well,   I crossed the desert, reaching higher ground,
               D♭   **A♭**   **D♭**   **A♭**

           D♭   **A♭**   **D♭**   **A♭**
then I pound the pavement to take the liars   down.

        D♭   **A♭**   **D♭**   **A♭**
But it's gone   forever, but never   too late,

           D♭ **A♭**   **D♭**   **A♭**
where the ever after is in the hands of fate.

          D♭   **G♭**   **D♭**   **A♭**   **D♭ A♭**
Chorus: Well, I, I just want   to see the light.

           D♭   **G♭**   **D♭**   **A♭**   **D♭ A♭**
And I, I don't want to lose my sight.

          D♭   **G♭**   **D♭**   **A♭**   **D♭ A♭**
Well, I, I just want   to see the light.

       D♭   **G♭**   **D♭**   **E♭** | **A♭** **E♭** **A♭** **C** ‖
And I need to know what's worth the fight.

Repeat and fade

Outro:

SHE

Lyrics by BILLIE JOE
Music by GREEN DAY

To match recording,
tune down 1/2 step:
⑥ = E♭   ③ = G♭
⑤ = A♭   ② = B♭
④ = D♭   ① = E♭

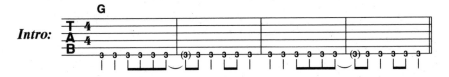

Intro:

Verse 1:
G
She, she screams in silence.
D

C
A sullen riot penetrating through her mind.
G

D
Waiting for a sign

C
To smash the silence with the brick of self-control.
G

Chorus:
D
Are you locked up in a world that's

C
been planned out for you?
G

D   C   G
Are you feeling like a social tool without a use?

C   G   C   G
Scream at me until my ears bleed.

C   G   D
I'm taking heed just for you.

Verse 2:
G   D
She, she's figured out

C   G   C G
All her doubts were someone else's point of view.

D
Waking up this time

C   G   C   G
To smash the silence with the brick of self-control.

Chorus:

    D
Are you locked up in a world that's

C   **G**
been planned out for you?

D   **C**   **G**
Are you feeling like a social tool without a use?

C   **G**   **C**   **G**
Scream at me until my ears bleed.

      C   **G**   **D**
I'm taking heed just for you.

Interlude:

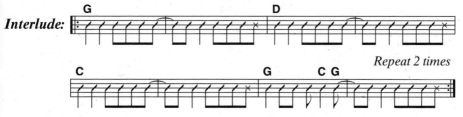

Repeat 2 times

Chorus:

    D
Are you locked up in a world that's

C   **G**
been planned out for you?

D   **C**   **G**
Are you feeling like a social tool without a use?

C   **G**   **C**   **G**
Scream at me until my ears bleed.

      C   **G**   **D**   **G**
I'm taking heed just for you.

SHE'S A REBEL

Words by BILLIE JOE
Music by GREEN DAY

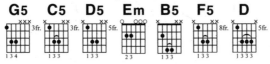

G5   C5   D5   Em   B5   F5   D

Chorus:

  G5
She's a rebel, she's a saint,

               D5   C5
she's the salt of the earth and she's dangerous.

  G5
She's a rebel, vigilante,

               D5   C5
missing link on the brink of destruction.

Verse 1:

G5   C5   G5   C5
From Chicago to Toronto,

G5   C5   D5   C5
she's the one that they call "old what's'ername."

G5   C5   G5   C5
She's the symbol of resistance,

G5   C5   D5   C5
and she's holding on my heart like a hand grenade.

|G5   C5 |G5   C5 |G5   C5 |D5   C5   ‖

Verse 2:

G5   C5   G5   C5
Is she dreaming what I'm thinking?

G5   C5   D5   C5
Is she the mother of all bombs gonna detonate?

G5   C5   G5   C5
Is she trouble like I'm trouble?

G5   C5   D5   C5
Make it a double twist of fate or a melody that

Bridge:

Em   B5   C5   G5
she sings. The revolution, the dawning of our lives.

C5   B5   Em   F5   D
She brings this liberation that I just can't define.

B5   A5   C5   G5 D5
Well, nothing comes to mind. Yeah.

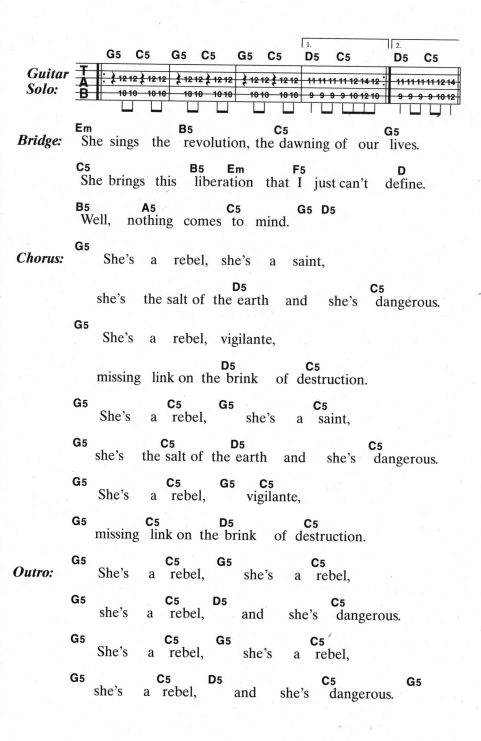

Guitar Solo:

| | G5 | C5 | G5 | C5 | G5 | C5 | D5 | C5 | D5 | C5 |

Bridge:

     Em   B5   C5   G5

She sings the revolution, the dawning of our lives.

  C5   B5   Em   F5   D

She brings this liberation that I just can't define.

  B5   A5   C5   G5 D5

Well, nothing comes to mind.

Chorus:

  G5

     She's a rebel, she's a saint,

                   D5   C5

    she's the salt of the earth and she's dangerous.

  G5

     She's a rebel, vigilante,

                   D5   C5

missing link on the brink of destruction.

  G5   C5   G5   C5

     She's a rebel, she's a saint,

  G5   C5   D5   C5

  she's the salt of the earth and she's dangerous.

  G5   C5   G5   C5

     She's a rebel, vigilante,

  G5   C5   D5   C5

missing link on the brink of destruction.

Outro:

  G5   C5   G5   C5

     She's a rebel, she's a rebel,

  G5   C5   D5   C5

  she's a rebel, and she's dangerous.

  G5   C5   G5   C5

     She's a rebel, she's a rebel,

  G5   C5   D5   C5   G5

  she's a rebel, and she's dangerous.

ST. JIMMY

Words by BILLIE JOE
Music by GREEN DAY

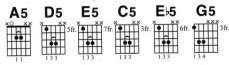

A5 D5 E5 C5 E♭5 G5

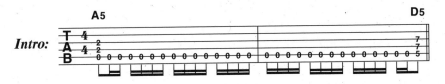

Intro:

A5   D5

Verse 1:

    A5   D5

Saint   Jimmy's coming down across the alleyway.

    A5   D5

Up on the boulevard like a zip gun on parade.

    A5   D5 A5   D5

Lights of a silhouette,   he's insubordinate.

    A5   D5

Coming at you on the count of

E5   D5   **N.C.**

one two...   one, two, three, four!

Riff A- -

A5   D5   E5   A5

Interlude:

Verse 2:

    A5   D5   E5   A5

My name is Jimmy and you'd better not wear it out.

                  D5   E5   A5

Suicide commando that your momma talked about.

                  D5   E5   A5

King of the forty thieves and I'm here to represent

                 D5   E5   A5

the needle in the vein of the establishment.

             D5   A5

Pre-chorus: I'm the patron saint of the denial

             D5   E5

with an angel face and a taste for suicidal.

w/Riff A

‖: **A5**   **D5** | | **E5**   **A5** | :‖

A5   **D5**   **E5**   **A5**
Verse 3:   Cigarettes and ramen and a little bag of dope.

                  D5   **E5**   **A5**
        I   am the son of a bitch and Edgar Allan Poe.

                  D5   **E5**   **A5**
        Raised in the city in the hail of lights,

                  D5   **E5**   **A5**
        product of war and fear that we've been victimized.

                       D5   **A5**
Pre-chorus: I'm the patron saint of the denial

                   D5   **E5**
        with an angel face and a taste for suicidal.

Riff B - ⌐
A5   **D5** **A5**   **D5** **E5**

Interlude:

w/Riff B, 3 times
A5 **D5** **A5** **D5** **E5**
                            Are you talking to me?
A5 **D5** **A5** **D5** **E5**

A5 **D5** **A5** **D5** **E5**
                            I'll give you something to cry about.

A5   **E5**   **C5**   **E♭5**   *Repeat 4 times*

                            (4th time) Saint Jimmy!
A5   **D5**   **E5**   **A5**

A5   **D5**   **E5**

A5   **D5**   **G5**   **D5**   **A5**

148

Verse 4:
A5
My name is Saint Jimmy, I'm a   **D5** son of a gun,

        G5   **D5**   **A5**
I'm the one that's from the way outside now. (Saint Jimmy.)

            D5   **G5**
A teenage assassin executing some fun in the cult

    D5   **A5**
of the life of crime, now. (Saint Jimmy.)

                     D5
I'd really hate to say it but I told you so, so shut

    G5   **D5**   **A5**
your mouth before I shoot you down, ol' boy.(Saint Jimmy.)

              D5
Welcome to the club and give me some blood, I'm the

G5   **D5**   **A5**
resident leader of the lost and found. (Saint Jimmy.)

       A5 **D5**   **E5** **A5**
Outro: It's comedy and tragedy.

           D5   **E5**   **A5**
It's Saint Jimmy, and that's my name,

                    A5
and don't wear it out.

THE STATIC AGE

Lyrics by BILLIE JOE
Music by GREEN DAY

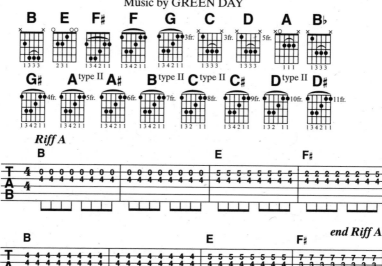

Riff A

Intro:

B

E

F#

end Riff A

B

E

F#

Verse 1:

B w/Riff A, 2 times

Can you hear the sound of the static noise,

E

F#
blasting out in stereo?

B
Cater to the class and the paranoid,

E

F#
music to my nervous system.

B
Advertising love and religion,

E

F#
murder on the airwaves.

B
Slogans on the brink of corruption,

E

F#
visions of blasphemy, war and peace, oh, screaming at you.

Chorus:

B   E   F#
I can't see a thing in the video.

B   E   F#
I can't hear a sound on the radio

B   E   F#   B   F#
in stereo in the static age.

150

w/Riff A

| B | | | E | F♯ | B | | | E | F♯ | ‖

Verse 2: B *w/Riff A, 2 times*   E
Billboard on the rise in the dawn's landscape,

            F♯
working your insanity.

B   E
Tragic à la madness and concrete,

Coca   Cola   F♯
            execution.

B   E
Conscience on a cross and your heart's in a vice,

                F♯
squeezing out your state of mind;

B
are what you own that you cannot E
                         buy?

           F♯
What a fucking tragedy, strategy, oh, screaming at you.

Chorus: B   E   F♯
I can't see a thing in the video.

B   E   F♯
I can't hear a sound on the radio

B   E F♯   B   F♯
in stereo in the static age.

B   E   F♯
I can't see a thing in the video.

B   E   F♯
I can't hear a sound on the radio

B   E F♯   B
in stereo in the static age.

Bridge: E
Hey, hey, it's the static age.

           B
Well, this is how the west was won.

E   F♯ F F♯ G
Hey, hey, it's the static age millennium.

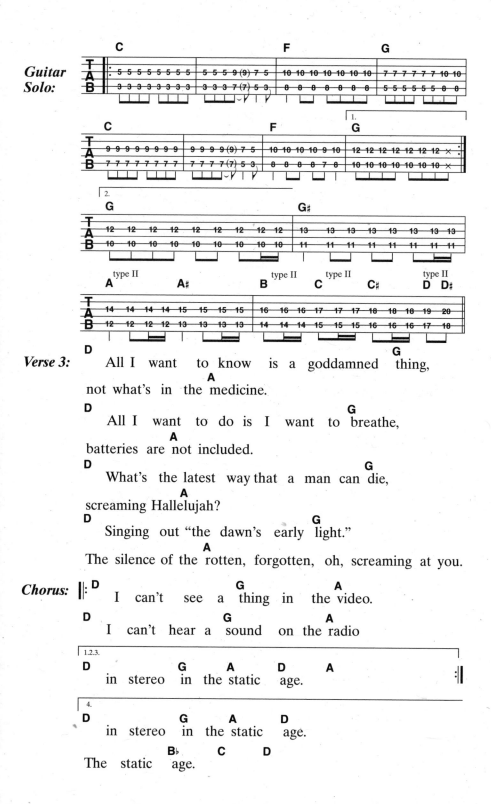

Guitar Solo:

Verse 3:
All I want to know is a goddamned thing,
not what's in the medicine.
All I want to do is I want to breathe,
batteries are not included.
What's the latest way that a man can die,
screaming Hallelujah?
Singing out "the dawn's early light."
The silence of the rotten, forgotten, oh, screaming at you.

Chorus:
I can't see a thing in the video.
I can't hear a sound on the radio

1.2.3.
in stereo in the static age.

4.
in stereo in the static age.
The static age.

STUCK WITH ME

Lyrics by BILLIE JOE
Music by BILLIE JOE and GREEN DAY

To match recording,
tune down 1/2 step:
⑥ = E♭   ③ = G♭
⑤ = A♭   ② = B♭
④ = D♭   ① = E♭

Intro:

| E | | C♯ B A | |

Verse 1:

      E   **B**
I'm not part of your elite, I'm just alright.

  A   **B**   **A**   **B**
Class structures waving colors, bleeding from my throat.

  E   **B**
Not subservient to you, I'm just alright.

  A   **B**   **A**   **B**
Down classed by the powers that be, give me loss of hope.

Chorus:

C♯m   **A**   **E**
Cast out, buried in a hole.

C♯m   **A**   **E**
Struck down, forcing me to fall.

C♯m   **A**   **E**
Destroyed, giving up the fight.

         A   **B** **E**
Well, I know I'm not alright.

Verse 2:

E   **B**
What's my price and will you pay it if it's alright?

A   **B**   **A**   **B**
Take it from my dignity and waste it 'til it's dead.

E   **B**
Throw me back into the gutter 'cause it's alright.

A   **B**   **A**   **B**
Find another pleasure f***er, drag them down to hell.

C♯m   **A**   **E**

Chorus: Cast   out,   buried in a hole.

C♯m   **A**   **E**

Struck down, forcing me to fall.

C♯m   **A**   **E**

Destroyed, giving up the fight.

        A   **B**   **E**

Well,   I   know I'm not alright.

Repeat 4 times

Interlude:

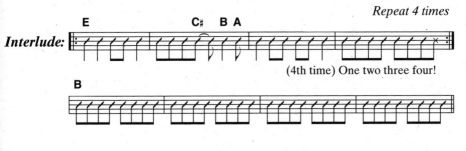

(4th time) One two three four!

C♯m   **A**   **E**

Chorus: Cast   out,   buried in a hole.

C♯m   **A**   **E**

Struck down, forcing me to fall.

C♯m   **A**   **E**

Destroyed,   giving up the fight.

        A   **B**   **E**

Well,   I   know I'm not alright.

UPTIGHT

Lyrics by BILLIE JOE
Music by BILLIE JOE and GREEN DAY

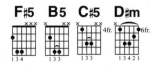

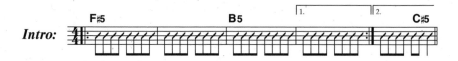

Intro:

F#5   B5   [1.]   [2.]   C#5

Verse 1:
                  B5
I woke up on the wrong side of the floor.

F#5   **B5**
Made, made my way through the front door.

F#5   **B5**
Broke my engagement with myself.

        C#5   **B5**
Pre-chorus: Perfect picture of bad health.

         C#5   **B5**
Another notch scratched on my belt.

         C#5   **B5**
The future just ain't what it used to be.

Interlude: | F#5 | B5 | F#5 | B5 | C#5 ||

        F#5   **B5**
Verse 2: I got a new start on a dead - end road.

F#5   **B5**
Peaked, peaked out on reaching new lows.

F#5   **B5**
Owed, paid up all my debts to myself.

        C#5   **B5**
Pre-chorus: Perfect picture of bad health.

         C#5   **B5**
Another notch scratched on my belt.

         C#5   **B5**
The future's in my living room.

Chorus: ‖: **F♯5** **B5**
Uptight, I'm a nag with a gun, yeah.

F♯5 **B5**
All night, suicide's last call.

F♯5 **C♯5**
I've been uptight, all night,

Repeat 2 times

F♯5 **B5 C♯5**
I'm a son of a gun. :‖

Guitar Solo:

F♯5

```
T
A  |: 11  11  11  10  10  10  11  11 | 11  10  10  10  11  11  10  10 |
B      9   9   9   8   8   8   9   9    9   8   8   8   9   9   8   8
```

Repeat 4 times

B5

```
T
A   11  11  11  10  10  10  11  11 | 11  10  10  10  11  11  10  10 :|
B    9   9   9   8   8   8   9   9    9   8   8   8   9   9   8   8
```

Chorus: ‖: **F♯5** **B5**
Uptight, I'm nag with a gun, yeah.

F♯5 **B5**
All night, suicide's last call.

F♯5 **C♯5**
I've been uptight, all night,

Repeat 4 times

F♯5 **B5 C♯5**
I'm a son of a gun. :‖ **D♯m** ‖

¡VIVA LA GLORIA!

Lyrics by BILLIE JOE
Music by GREEN DAY

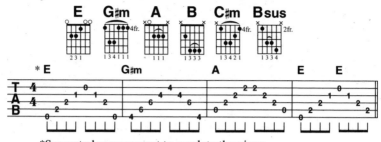

*Suggested arrangement to emulate the piano.

	E	G#m	A	E
Intro:	Hey, Gloria, are you	standing	close to	the edge?

                               G#m
Look   out to the setting sun,

A   **B**
the brink of your vision.

E   **G#m**   **A**   **E**
Eternal youth is a landscape of a lie.

                         G#m
The cracks of my skin can prove,

A   **B**
as the years will testify.

C#m   **G#m**
Say your prayers and light a fire.

A   **E**   **B**
We're gonna start a war.

C#m   **G#m**
Your slogan's a gun for hire.

A   **B**
It's what we've waited for.

E   **G#m**   **A**   **E**
Hey, Gloria, this is why we're on the edge.

                         G#m
The fight of our lives been drawn to

A   **E**
this undying love.

       E   G♯m

Chorus: Gloria, viva   la Gloria.

C♯m   A

You   blast your   name in graffiti on the walls.

Falling through broken glass   that's

E   B   C♯m

slashing   through your   spirit.

A   B

I can hear it like   a jilted crowd.

E   G♯m

Gloria, where are you,   Gloria?

C♯m

You   found a   home in all your

A

scars and   ammunition.

You   made   your   bed in salad

E   B   C♯m

days amongst the   ruins.

A   B

Ashes to ashes of our   youth.

E   G♯m   C♯m

Verse: She   smashed her knuckles into   winter.

A   E   B

As   autumn's wind fades into   black.

E   G♯m   C♯m

She   is the   saint of all the   sinners,

A   E   B

The one that's fallen through the   cracks.

              A   B

So don't put away your   burning light.

        E   G♯m

Chorus: Gloria, where are you,   Gloria?

       C♯m   A

        Don't lose your   faith to your   lost   naiveté.

        Weather   the storm and   don't look

       E   B   C♯m

back   on last   November,

       A   B

        When your banners were burning down.

       E   G♯m

       Gloria, viva   la   Gloria.

       C♯m   A

        Send me your amnesty down to the broken hearted.

                                  E   B   C♯m

        Bring us the season that we always will   remember.

         A   B

         Don't let the bonfires   go out.

         A   E A   E

Outro: So, Gloria,   send   out your   message of

       A   E   B   Bsus B

        the light   that   shadows in the night.

       A   E A   E

Gloria,   where's your undying love?

       A   E   B   E

        Tell me the story of your   life   your   life.

¿VIVA LA GLORIA? (LITTLE GIRL)

Lyrics by BILLIE JOE
Music by GREEN DAY

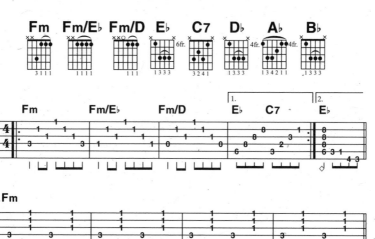

Intro:

Fm

Verse 1:

       Fm   **Db**
Little   girl, little   girl,   why are you crying?

     C7   **Fm**
Inside your   restless soul   your   heart is dying.

                                Db
Little one, little   one,   your   soul   is purging,

     C7   **Fm**
Of love   and   razor blades your   blood is surging.

Chorus:

                           Db
Run   away   from   the   river   to the street

     C7   **Fm**
and   find   yourself with   your   face in the gutter.

                    Db
You're a   stray   for the Salvation Army.

     C7
There is no place   like home

                    Fm
when   you got no place   to go.

Verse 2: Little   girl,   little   girl,   your   life is calling the
                                                          Db

C7   **Fm**
charlatans and saints   of your   abandon.

Little   one,   little   one,   the sky is falling.
Db

C7   **Fm**
Your   lifeboat of deception is now sailing.

                                   Db
In the wake   all the way no rhyme   or reason,

        C7   **Fm**
Your bloodshot eyes will show   your   heart of   treason.

                                    Db
Little   girl,   little   girl,   you   dirty liar.

       C7   **Fm**
You're just a junkie preaching to the choir.

                             Db
Chorus: Run   away   from   the   river to the street

         C7   **Fm**
and   find   yourself with   your   face in the gutter.

                        Db
You're a   stray   for the Salvation Army.

          C7
There is   no place   like home

                     Fm
when   you got no place   to go.

       Db   **Ab**
Bridge: The   traces of blood always follow you   home

               Db   **Ab**
like   the   mascara   tears from your   getaway.

             Db   **Ab**
You're walking with blisters and   running   with shears.

       C7   **Fm**
So unholy sister   of grace.

Guitar Solo: ‖: Fm | | Fm/E♭ | | Fm/D | B♭ | E♭ | C7 :‖ C7 ‖

1.2.3. | 4.

Chorus:

                                         D♭

Run   away   from   the   river   to the street

          C7   **Fm**

and   find   yourself with   your   face in the gutter.

                            D♭

You're a stray   for the Salvation Army.

          C7

There is no place like   home...

Outro:

N.C.

```
T|---------------------------|
A|---------------------------|
B|--3---1-----------------|
        --4---3--
```

162

WAITING

Lyrics by BILLIE JOE
Music by GREEN DAY

To match recording,
tune down 1/2 step:
⑥ = E♭　③ = G♭
⑤ = A♭　② = B♭
④ = D♭　① = E♭

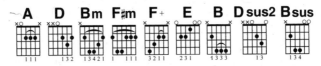

A　　D
Intro: I've　been　waiting a　long　time

Bm　　　D
for this　moment　to　come.

A　　　D　　　　　Bm　　D
I'm destined　for anything at　all.

A　　　D
Verse 1: Downtown　lights　will be　shining

Bm　　D
on me like a　new　diamond

A　　　D　　　　　Bm　　　D
ring out under　the midnight　hour.

A　　　D
Well,　no　one　can　touch　me now.

Bm　　　　D
And　I　can't　turn　my　back,

A　　　D　　　　Bm　　D
it's　too late,　ready　or　not at　all.

F♯m　　　　F+　　　　E　　　　　B
Chorus: Well,　I'm so　much　closer than　I　have　ever　known.

D　　A　　　D

Wake up.

A　　D
Verse 2: Dawning　of　a　new　era.

Bm　　D
Calling,　don't　let it　catch　you

A　　　D　　　　　Bm　　D
falling,　ready　or not at　all.

A　　　D
Well,　so　close,　enough to　taste　it.

Bm   **D**
Almost I can embrace this feeling

A

D
on the tip of my tongue.

Bm   **D**

Chorus: Well, I'm so much closer than I have ever known.

F#m   **F+**   **E**   **B**

Wake up.

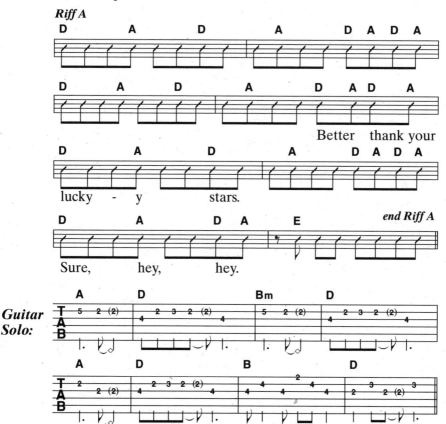

Riff A

Better thank your lucky-y stars.

Sure, hey, hey.

Guitar Solo:

Chorus: Well, I'm so much closer than I have ever known.

F#m   **F+**   **E**   **B**

Wake up.

D *w/Riff A*
Better thank your lucky - stars.

E
Sure, hey, hey, hey.

Interlude:

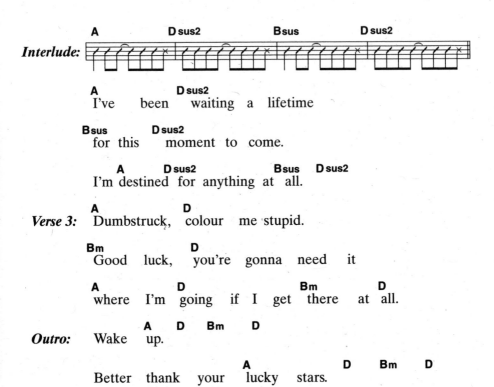

A   D sus2
I've   been   waiting   a   lifetime

Bsus   D sus2
for this   moment to come.

A   D sus2   Bsus   D sus2
I'm destined for anything at all.

A   D
Verse 3: Dumbstruck, colour   me stupid.

Bm   D
Good   luck,   you're   gonna   need   it

A   D   Bm   D
where I'm going if I get there   at all.

A   D   Bm   D
Outro: Wake   up.

A   D   Bm   D
Better thank your   lucky   stars.

WARNING

Words by BILLIE JOE
Music by GREEN DAY

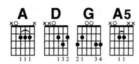

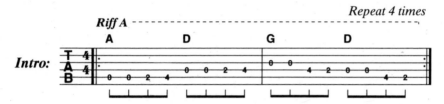

Intro:

w/Riff A, 8 times

            A   **D**

Verse 1: This   is a public service announcement.

G   **D**   **A D G D**
This   is only   a   test.

    A   **D**   **G**   **D**   **A D G D**
Emergency, evacuation, protest.

       A   **D**   **G**   **D**
May impair your ability to operate machinery.

A   **D** **G**   **D**
Can't quite tell just what it means to me.

A   **D**
Keep out of reach of children,

G   **D**
Don't you talk to strangers.

        A   **D**   **G**   **D**
Get your philosophy from a bumper sticker.

w/Riff A, 4 times

A **D** **G**   **D**   **A D G D**
Chorus: Warning: Live without warning.

           A **D** **G**   **D**
Let's see a warning: Live without warning.

A **D** **G**   **D**
         Without.   Alright.

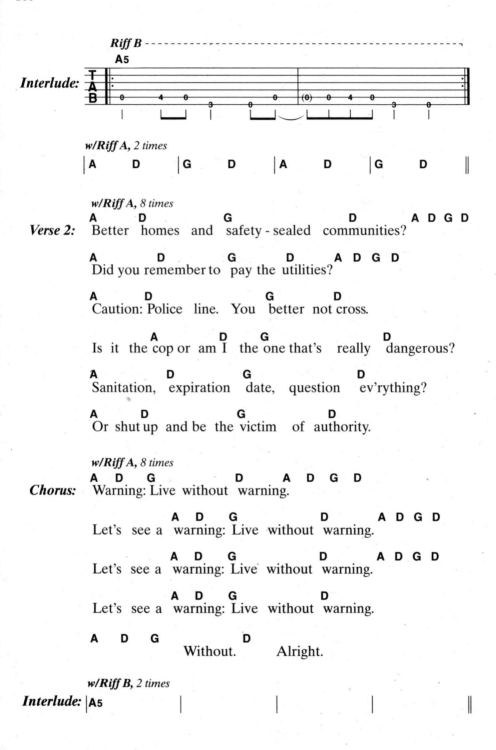

Riff B -

A5

Interlude:

w/**Riff A,** 2 times

| A | D | G | D | A | D | G | D |

w/**Riff A,** 8 times

A   D   G   D   A D G D

Verse 2:   Better homes and safety - sealed communities?

A   D   G   D   A D G D

Did you remember to pay the utilities?

A   D   G   D

Caution: Police line. You better not cross.

            A   D   G   D

Is it the cop or am I the one that's really dangerous?

A   D   G   D

Sanitation, expiration date, question ev'rything?

A   D   G   D

Or shut up and be the victim of authority.

w/**Riff A,** 8 times

A   D   G   D   A   D   G   D

Chorus: Warning: Live without warning.

            A   D   G   D   A D G D

Let's see a warning: Live without warning.

            A   D   G   D   A D G D

Let's see a warning: Live without warning.

            A   D   G   D

Let's see a warning: Live without warning.

A   D   G   D

           Without.   Alright.

w/**Riff B,** 2 times

Interlude: | A5 | | | ‖

w/Riff B, 4 times
A5
Verse 3: Better homes and safety - sealed communities?

Did you remember to pay the utilities?

w/Riff A, 4 times
A   **D**   **G**   **D**
Caution: Police line. You better not cross.

          A   **D**   **G**   **D**
Is it the cop or am I the one that's really dangerous?

A   **D**   **G**   **D**
Sanitation, expiration date, question ev'rything?

A   **D**   **G**   **D**
Or shut up and be the victim of authority.

w/Riff A, 8 times
A   **D G**   **D**   **A D G D**
Chorus: Warning: Live without warning.

              A   **D**   **G**   **D**   **A D G D**
Let's see a warning: Live without warning.

              A   **D**   **G**   **D**   **A D G D**
Let's see a warning: Live without warning.

             A   **D**   **G**   **D**   **A**   **D**   **G**   **D**
Let's see a warning: Live without warning.

           w/Riff A
           A   **D**
Outro: This is a public service announcement.

G   **D**   **A**
This is only a test.

WAKE ME UP WHEN SEPTEMBER ENDS

Words by BILLIE JOE
Music by GREEN DAY

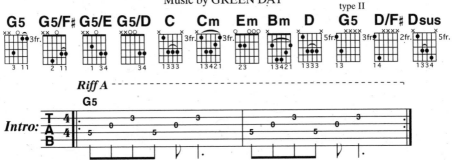

Riff A -

Intro:

Verse 1:

G5   G5/F♯
Summer has come   and passed,

    G5/E   G5/D
the innocent can never   last.

C   Cm   G5
Wake   me up when   September   ends.

               G5/F♯
Like   my father's come   to pass,

G5/E
seven   years   has   G5/D gone   so fast.

C   Cm   G5
Wake   me up when   September   ends.

Chorus:

Em   Bm   C   G5   G5/F♯
Here   comes   the rain again, falling   from   the stars.

Em   Bm   C   D
Drenched in my pain again, becoming who we are.

Verse 2:

G5   G5/F♯   G5/E   G5/D
As my memory rests,   but never   forgets   what   I   lost.

C   Cm   G5
Wake   me up   when   September   ends.

w/ Riff A, 3 times

Interlude: |G5 | | | | | ‖

Verse 3:

G5   G5/F♯
Summer has come and passed,

    G5/E   G5/D
the innocent can never   last.

C   Cm   G5 type II
Wake   me up when   September   ends.

G5   **G5/F♯**
Ring   out the bells   again,

G5/E   **G5/D**
like   we did when   spring   began.

C   **Cm**   type II
                                            G5   **D/F♯**
Wake me up when   September ends.

Chorus:

Em   **Bm**   **C**   type II
                                          G5 **D/F♯**
Here   comes   the rain again,   falling   from   the stars.

Em   **Bm**   **C**   **D**
Drenched in my pain again, becoming who we are.

Verse 4:

G5   **G5/F♯**   **G5/E**   **G5/D**
As my memory rests,   but never   forgets   what   I   lost.

C   **Cm**   type II
                                        G5   **D/F♯**
Wake me up   when September   ends.

Guitar Solo:

w/Riff A, *2 times*

Interlude: |G5 | | | ‖

Verse 5:

G5   **G5/F♯**
Summer has   come   and passed,

    G5/E   **G5/D**
the innocent can never   last.

C   **Cm**   type II
                                        G5
Wake me up when September   ends.

G5   **G5/F♯**
Like   my father's come   to pass,

G5/E   **G5/D**
twenty years   has   gone   so fast.

Repeat 3 times

                                      type II
‖: **C**   **Cm**   **G5**
   Wake me up when September ends.   :‖

WALKING CONTRADICTION

Lyrics by BILLIE JOE
Music by GREEN DAY

To match recording,
tune down 1/2 step:
⑥ = E♭   ③ = G♭
⑤ = A♭   ② = B♭
④ = D♭   ① = E♭

A   **D**   **G**

Intro: 4/4

	A		D	G	A
Verse 1:	Do as I	say,	not as I	do	

                                                 D   **G**   **A**
because the s***'s so deep   you can't run away.

                D   **G**   **A**
I beg to differ,   on the contrary,

                D   **G**   **A**
I agree with   ev'ry   word   that you say.

                D   **G**   **A**
Talk   is cheap   and lies are expensive,

                D   **G**   **A**
my wallet's   fat and so is   my head.

                D   **G**   **A**
Hit   and   run,   and   then,   I'll hit you again,

                D   **G**   **A**
a   smart   ass   but,   I'm playing   dumb.

Interlude:

A	D G	A	A	D G	A

	A	D	G	A
Verse 2:	Standards set and broken	all the time,

                D   **G**   **A**
Control the chaos   behind   the gun.

                D   **G**   **A**
Call   it as I   see it,   even   if

                D   **G**   **A**
I was   born   deaf,   blind,   and dumb.

              D   **G**   **A**
Losers   winning big on the lottery,

              D   **G**   **A**
Rehab   rejects   still sniffing   glue.

       D **G**   **A**
Constant refutation with myself,

              D   **G**   **A**
I'm a   victim of a   catch 22.

       D **G** **A**
Chorus: I have   no belief,

       D **G** **A**   **D**   **G**   **A**
But I believe I'm a walking contradiction.

         D   **G**   **A**
And   I ain't   got no right.

Interlude:

   A   **D**   **G**   **A**
Verse 3: Do as I say,   not as I   do

                 D   **G**   **A**
because the s***'s so deep you can't run away.

         D   **G**   **A**
I beg to differ,   on the contrary,

             D   **G**   **A**
I agree with   ev'ry   word that you say.

           D   **G**   **A**
Talk   is cheap and lies are expensive,

           D   **G**   **A**
my wallet's fat and so is my head.

           D   **G**   **A**
Hit   and   run,   and   then, I'll hit you again,

          D   **G**   **A**
a smart   ass   but,   I'm playing dumb.

       D **G** **A**
Chorus: ||:   I have   no belief,

       D **G** **A**   **D**   **G**   **A**
But I believe I'm a walking contradiction.

                        Repeat chorus 2 times
         D   **G**   **A**
And   I ain't   got no right.   :||

Outro:

WELCOME TO PARADISE

Lyrics by BILLIE JOE
Music by GREEN DAY

To match recording,
tune down 1/2 step:
⑥ = E♭ ③ = G♭
⑤ = A♭ ② = B♭
④ = D♭ ① = E♭

type II

E   D   A   G   C   B   G   F#   F

Repeat 4 times

Riff A -

E   D   A

Intro: 4/4

Verse 1:
E   D   E
Dear   mother, can you hear me whining?

D
It's   been   three   whole   weeks   since   that

G   B
I   have   left   your   home.

E   D   E
This sudden fear has left me trembling

D
'Cause   now it   seems   that I   am

G   B   G   B
out here on my own   And I'm feeling so   alone.

Chorus:
E   G   A   C
Pay attention to the cracked streets and the broken homes.

E   G   B
Some call it slums, some call it nice.

E   G
I want to take you through a   wasteland

A   C
I'd   like to call my own.

w/Riff A, 2 times
E B   E   D A E D A
Welcome to paradise.

Verse 2:
E   D   E
A gunshot rings out at the station,

D   G   B
Another urchin snaps and left dead on his own.

E   D   E
It makes me wonder why I'm still here.

D   G   B
For some strange reason, it's now feeling like my home,

          G   **B**
And I'm never gonna go.

       E   **G**   **A**   **C**
Chorus: Pay attention to the cracked streets and the broken homes.

       E   **G**   **B**
    Some call it slums, some call it nice.

        E   **G**
I want to take you through a wasteland

       A   **C**
I'd like to call my own.

                      w/Riff A, 4 times
  E B   **E**   **D A E D A E D A E D A**
   Welcome to paradise.

                                    Repeat 20 times

        E   **G** type II   **F♯**   **F**

```
        E         G type II       F#            F
T |----------9---------12--------|------11----------10-------|
A |:---9--9------12------12------|---11----11----10------10--|:
B |-7---------10----------------9---11--------8------10------|
```

Interlude:

        E   **D**   **E**
Verse 3: Dear   mother, can you hear me laughing?

                D
It's been   six whole months since   that

G   **B**
I have   left your home.

E   **D**   **E**
  It makes me wonder why I'm still here.

                   D   **G**   **B**
For some   strange reason, it's now feeling like my home,

           G   **B**
And I'm never   gonna go.

       E   **G**   **A**   **C**
Chorus: Pay attention to the cracked streets and the broken homes.

       E   **G**   **B**
    Some   call it slums, some   call it nice.

        E   **G**
I want to take you through a wasteland

       A   **C**
I'd like to call my own.

                    w/Riff A, 4 times
  E B   **E**   **D A E D A**
   Welcome to paradise.

          E   **D A E D A E**
Oh, paradise.

WHEN I COME AROUND

Lyrics by BILLIE JOE
Music by GREEN DAY

To match recording,
tune down 1/2 step:
⑥ = E♭ ③ = G♭
⑤ = A♭ ② = B♭
④ = D♭ ① = E♭

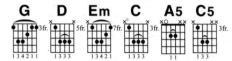

G   D   Em   C   A5   C5

Repeat 3 times

Riff A - ,

G   D   Em   C

Intro:

```
T  4 ‖:                    7   7 ×   8   8 × 5   5   5   5 ×
A  4        4  4 ×         7   7 ×   9   9 × 5   5   5   5 × :‖
B        5  5  5  5 × 7  7 7  7 ×   7   7 × 3   3   3   3 ×
      3  3  3  3 × 5  5 5  5 ×
```

Verse 1:

G   D   Em   C
I   heard   you   cryin'   loud

G   D   Em   C
all   the   way   across   town.

G   D
You've   been   searching   for   that   someone,

Em   C
And   it's   me,   out on   the   prowl.

G   D   Em   C
As   you   sit   around   feeling   sorry   for   yourself,

G   D   Em   C
Well,   don't   get   lonely   now

G   D   Em   C
and   dry   your   whining   eyes.

G   D   Em
I'm just roaming for the moment sleazing   my   back   yard,

C   G
So   don't   get   so   uptight,

D   Em   C
You   been   thinking   about   ditching   me.

Chorus:

A5   C5
No   time   to   search   the   world   around

A5   C5
'Cause   you   know   where   I'll   be   found

w/Riff A, 2 times

|G   D |Em   C |G   D |Em   C |
When I come around.

Verse 2:
```
          G       D              Em      C
          I   heard   it   all  before,

          G       D                      Em        C
          So  don't   knock   down   my door.

              G           D         Em              C
          I'm a  loser   and a  user so I   don't   need    no accuser

            G             D              Em          C
          To try and slag me down,   because I  know   you're  right.

          G       D              Em        C
          So  go  do  what   you  like.

          G       D              Em        C
          Make  sure  you do  it   wise.

                  G                      D
          You    may    find   out  that  your   self - doubt

                Em                  C
          means   nothing  was   ever  there.

                  G           D              Em        C
          You    can't  go forcing   something  if it's  just not right.
```

Chorus:
```
          A5                       C5
          No time    to  search   the world    around

          A5                            C5
          'Cause you  know   where  I'll  be  found
                           w/Riff A, 2 times
                         |G    D  |Em   C  |G    D  |Em  C  ‖
          When I come around. |        |        |        |   Ooh. ‖
```

```
      w/Riff A, 2 times
     |G       D       |Em    C     |G       D       |Em       C     ‖
```
Interlude:

Chorus:
```
          A5                       C5
          No time    to  search   the world    around

          A5                            C5
          'Cause  you know   where   I'll  be  found

          When      I     come       around.
```

```
      w/Riff A                                        Repeat 3 times
     ‖: G    D    Em    C                                          :‖
                          When   I   come     around.
```

```
      G                    D                Em              C
```

WHO WROTE HOLDEN CAULFIELD?

Lyrics by BILLIE JOE
Music by GREEN DAY

To match recording,
tune down 1/2 step:
⑥ = E♭ ③ = G♭
⑤ = A♭ ② = B♭
④ = D♭ ① = E♭

E5 D5 C#5 B5 F#m A E B D

Verse 1:

$\frac{4}{4}$ **E5**
A thought crossed in my head, **D5**

and I need to tell you;

C#5
It's news that I for thought. **B5**

E5 **D5**
Was it just a dream that happened long ago?

C#5
I think I just forgot. **B5**

Pre-chorus:

F#m
Well, it hasn't been the first time. **A**

F#m
And it sure does drive me mad. **A**

That's why I'm saying...

Chorus:

E **B** **D** **A**
There's a boy who fogs his world and now he's getting lazy.

E **B** **D** **A**
There's no motivation and frustration makes him crazy.

E **B** **D** **A**
He makes a plan to take a stand but always ends up sitting.

E **B** **D** **A**
Someone help him up or he is gonna end up quitting.

Verse 2:

E5 **D5** **C#5**
I shuffle through my mind to see if I can find

B5
the words I left behind.

E5 **D5**
Was it just a dream that happened long ago?

C#5 **B5**
Oh, well, never mind!

Pre-chorus:
F#m   A
Well, it hasn't been the first time.

F#m   A
And it sure does drive me mad.

That's why I'm saying...

Chorus:
E   B   D   A
There's a boy who fogs his world and now he's getting lazy.

E   B   D   A
There's no motivation and frustration makes him crazy.

E   B   D   A
He makes a plan to take a stand but always ends up sitting.

E   B   D   A
Someone help him up or he is gonna end up quitting.

Interlude:

E5 D5 C#5 B5 *Repeat 3 times*

E5 D5 C#5 B5

F#m A

(2nd time) That's why I'm saying...

Chorus:
E   B   D   A
There's a boy who fogs his world and now he's getting lazy.

E   B   D   A
There's no motivation and frustration makes him crazy.

E   B   D   A
He makes a plan to take a stand but always ends up sitting.

Repeat 2 times
E   B   D   A
Someone help him up or he is gonna end up quitting.

E

GUITAR
CHORD
GLOSSARY

A CHORDS

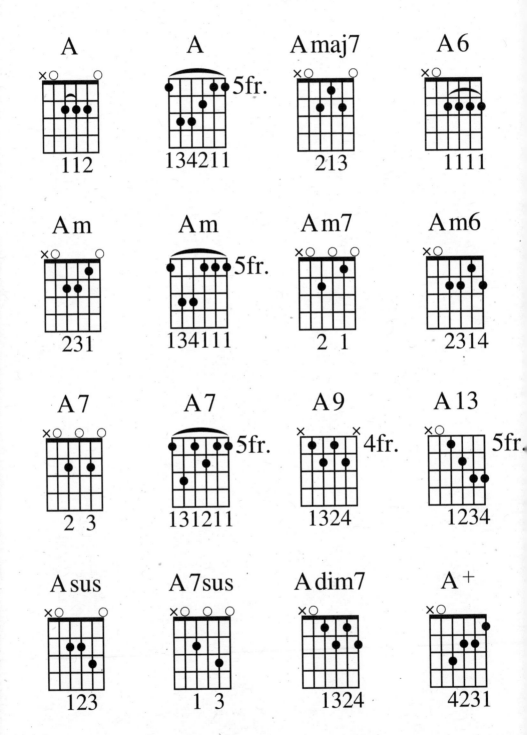

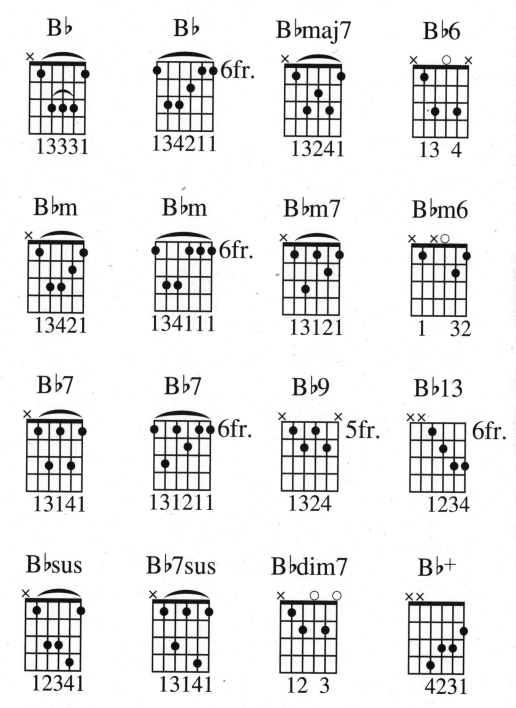

B CHORDS

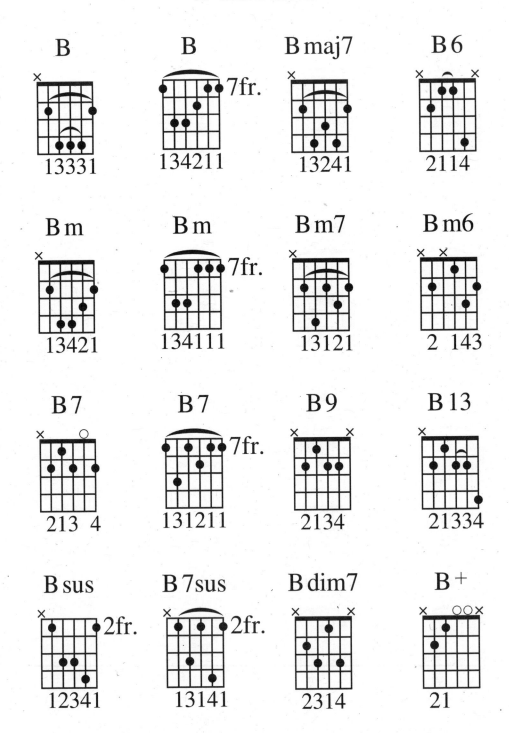

B
13331

B 7fr.
134211

B maj7
13241

B 6
2114

B m
13421

B m 7fr.
134111

B m7
13121

B m6
2 143

B 7
213 4

B 7 7fr.
131211

B 9
2134

B 13
21334

B sus 2fr.
12341

B 7sus 2fr.
13141

B dim7
2314

B +
21

C CHORDS

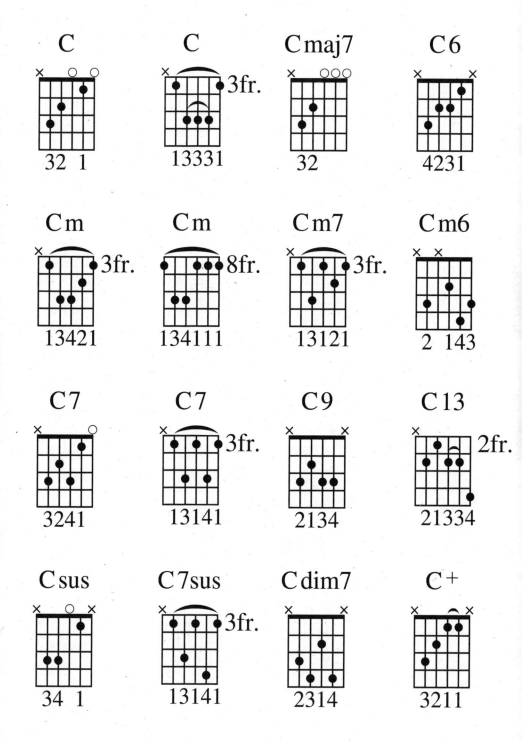

C# (D♭) CHORDS*

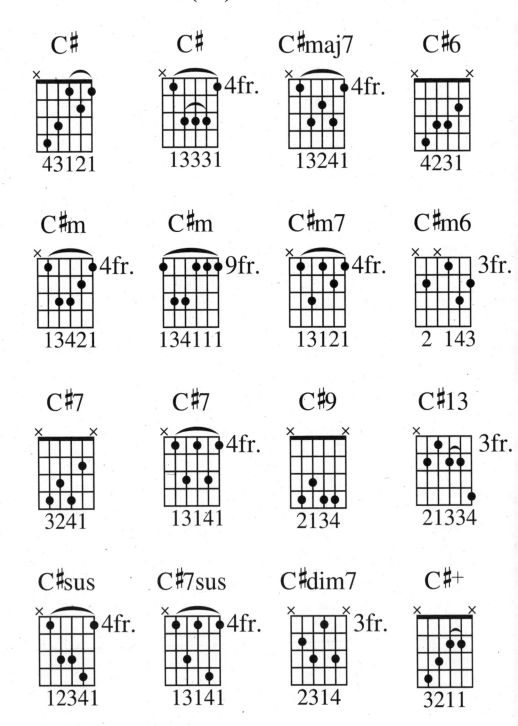

*C# and D♭ are two names for the same note.

D CHORDS

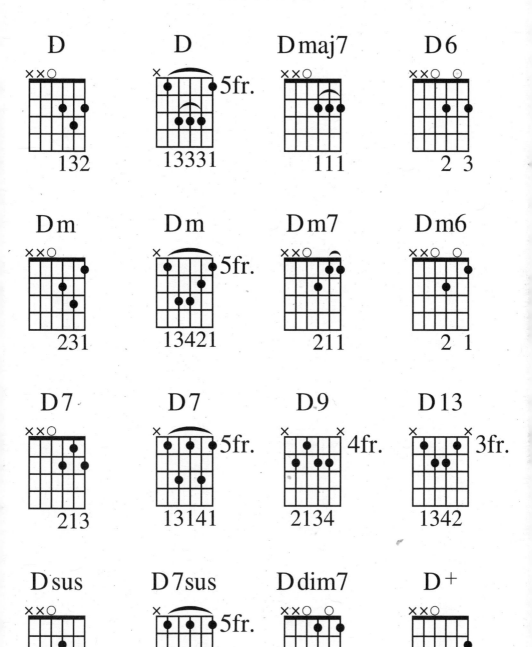

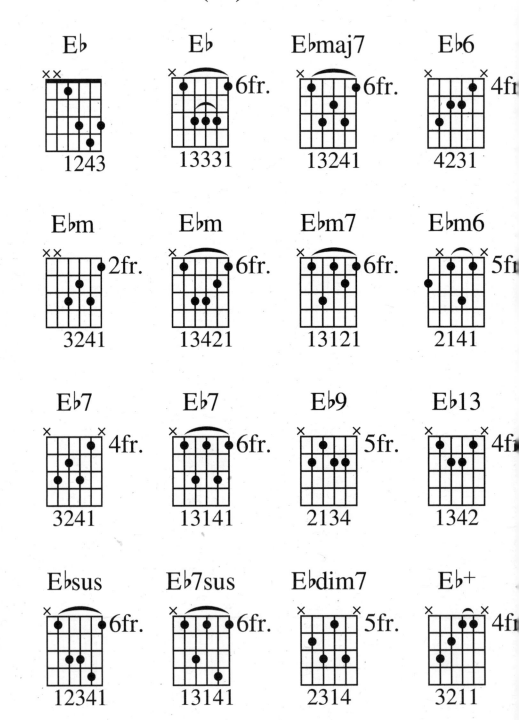

E♭ (D♯) CHORDS*

*E♭ and D♯ are two names for the same note.

E CHORDS

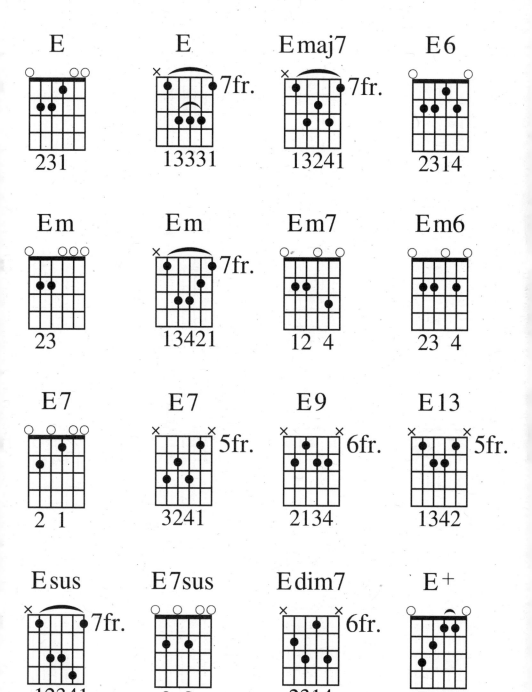

F CHORDS

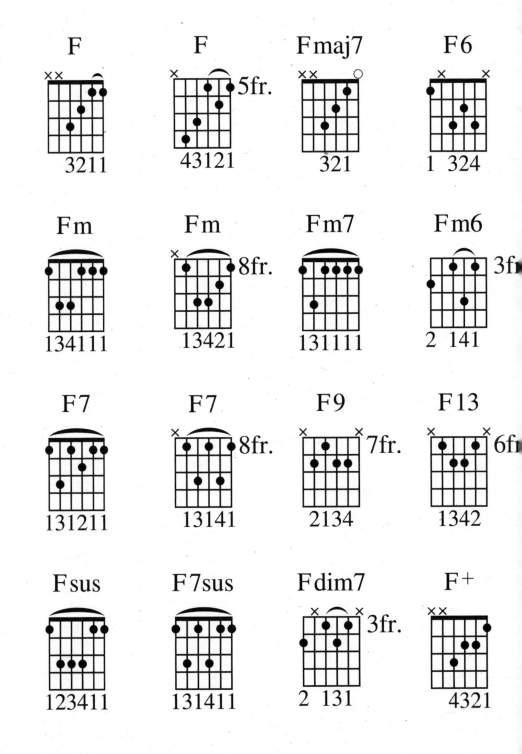

F♯ (G♭) CHORDS*

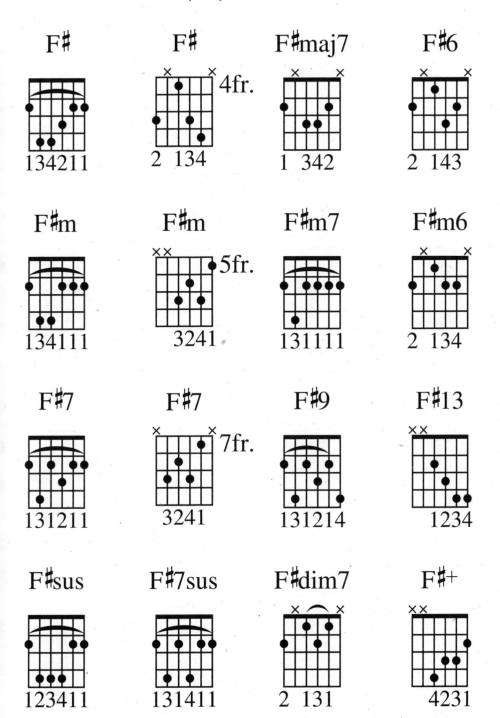

*F♯ and G♭ are two names for the same note.

G CHORDS

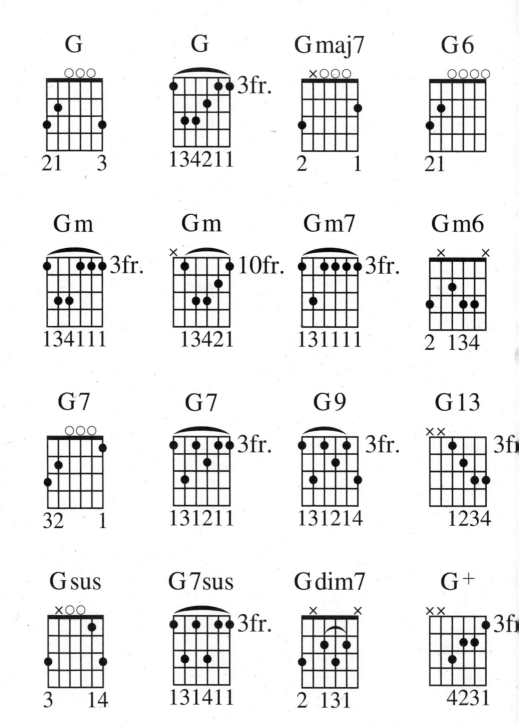

A♭ (G♯) CHORDS

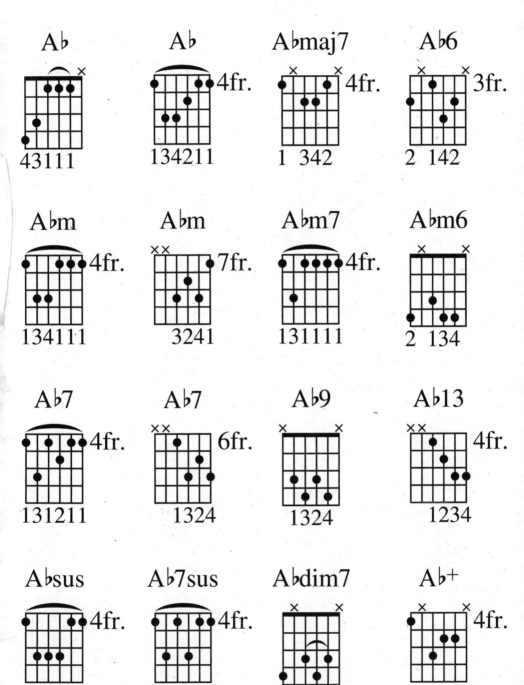

A♭ 43111

A♭ 4fr. 134211

A♭maj7 4fr. 1 342

A♭6 3fr. 2 142

A♭m 4fr. 134111

A♭m 7fr. 3241

A♭m7 4fr. 131111

A♭m6 2 134

A♭7 4fr. 131211

A♭7 6fr. 1324

A♭9 1324

A♭13 4fr. 1234

A♭sus 4fr. 123411

A♭7sus 4fr. 131411

A♭dim7 2 131

A♭+ 4fr. 1 423

*A♭ and G♯ are two names for the same note.